CREATIVE QUILTING
WITH BEADS

CREATIVE QUILTING WITH BEADS

20+ Projects with Dimension, Sparkle & Shine

Valerie Van Arsdale Shrader

LARK
CRAFTS

An Imprint of Sterling Publishing Co., Inc.
New York

WWW.LARKCRAFTS.COM

EDITOR:
Nathalie Mornu

TECHNICAL EDITOR:
Peggy Bendel

ART DIRECTOR:
828:design

COVER DESIGNER:
Cindy LaBreacht

ASSOCIATE ART DIRECTOR:
Shannon Yokeley

ART PRODUCTION ASSISTANT:
Jeff Hamilton

EDITORIAL ASSISTANCE:
Amanda Carestio, Dawn Dillingham

BASICS ILLUSTRATIONS
AND TEMPLATES:
Orrin Lundgren

PROJECT ILLUSTRATIONS:
Kara Gott

PHOTOGRAPHER:
Stewart O'Shields

The Library of Congress has cataloged the hardcover edition as follows:

Creative quilting with beads : bags, aprons, mini-quilts & more / edited by Peggy Bendel.
   p. cm.
  Includes index.
  ISBN-13: 978-1-60059-087-0 (hc-plc with jacket : alk. paper)
  ISBN-10: 1-60059-087-X (hc-plc with jacket : alk. paper)
 1. Patchwork--Patterns. 2. Quilting--Patterns. 3. Beadwork--Patterns.
I. Bendel, Peggy.
  TT835.C73965 2008
  746.46'041--dc22

                                      2007031078

10 9 8 7 6 5 4 3 2 1

Published by Lark Books, A Division of
Sterling Publishing Co., Inc.
387 Park Avenue South, New York, N.Y. 10016

First Paperback Edition 2012
Text © 2008, Lark Crafts, an Imprint of Sterling Publishing Co., Inc.
Photography © 2008, Lark Crafts, an Imprint of Sterling Publishing Co., Inc. unless otherwise specified
Illustrations © 2008, Lark Crafts, an Imprint of Sterling Publishing Co., Inc. unless otherwise specified

Distributed in Canada by Sterling Publishing,
c/o Canadian Manda Group, 165 Dufferin Street
Toronto, Ontario, Canada M6K 3H6

Distributed in the United Kingdom by GMC Distribution Services,
Castle Place, 166 High Street, Lewes, East Sussex, England BN7 1XU

Distributed in Australia by Capricorn Link (Australia) Pty Ltd.,
P.O. Box 704, Windsor, NSW 2756 Australia

If you have questions or comments about this book, please contact:
Lark Crafts
67 Broadway
Asheville, NC 28801
828-253-0467

Manufactured in China

ISBN 13: 978-1-60059-087-0 (hardcover) 978-1-4547-0336-5 (paperback)

For information about custom editions, special sales, premium and corporate purchases, please contact Sterling Special Sales Department at 800-805-5489 or specialsales@sterlingpub.com.

For information about desk and examination copies available to college and university professors, submit requests to academic@larkbooks.com. Our complete policy can be found at www.larkcrafts.com.

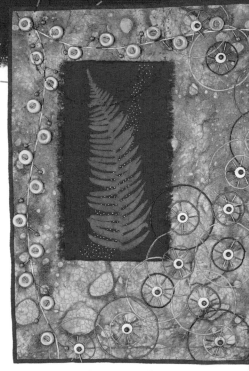

contents

INTRODUCTION

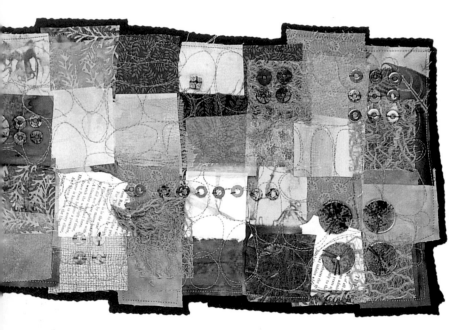

*A*re you a quilter inundated with piles of fabric scraps? Or perhaps a bead fanatic with tubs of fabulous beads looking for the right home? Whether you're searching for a new way to add texture (and sparkle) to your quilts or to expand your beading repertoire, *Creative Quilting with Beads* offers a wealth of design inspiration to take both mediums to a new level of radiance.

The 23 featured projects and an impressive gallery explore the many varied ways beads can work with their fabric backgrounds, either as part of a pattern or as a dramatic focal point. They also display an array of

beading approaches from extensive beadwork to more random applications. Beginning with simple designs that gradually combine more advanced techniques, the projects represent a wide range of artistic styles from the serene tones of Julie Donaldson's *Forest Fern Quilt* (page 76) and Kathy Daniels's subdued landscape *By the Sea* (page 26) to *Horror Vacui* (page 94), Jennifer Reis's dark and sophisticated art panel, and Heather Noblitt's intriguing *Latin Beauty* (page 34). Insightful words of wisdom from the designers themselves will aid and inspire the creative process. Each work is a unique expression of the designer's vision and offers

its own redefinition of quilting and beading, from traditional wall hangings to functional projects like purses, pillows, and book covers.

So what exactly constitutes a bead? Browse the projects and open your mind to the endless possibilities. How about using that treasured shell or bottle cap collection, or pieces of broken plates? You'll see how such items—even washers from the hardware store—can become dazzling beads and unique additions to both traditional and modern art quilts.

The basics section covers everything you'll need to get started. If you're new to beading, you'll find practical information on the different types of beads, ideas for finding them, and imaginative ways to create your own unique beads. Equipped with information on beading tools and supplies, you'll master basic beading stitches—and a few embroidery stitches— in no time. This section also provides an introduction to quilting materials, techniques, and stitches if you're a beginning quilter.

Ready to begin? Start with an easy project and then work on expanding your skills. Follow a project exactly or use a design as a jumping-off point for infusing new life into your quilts and your beads. No matter how you use this book, you'll gain invaluable skills in both beading and quilting, and you'll find an artistic way to use those leftover beads and fabric scraps.

the BASICS

lip through the pages of *Creative Quilting with Beads*, and you'll see that no two projects are alike. Our talented designers have combined the ancient crafts of beading and quilt making to create a variety of imaginative projects. Best of all, the designers share their techniques step-by-step, so you can join in the creative fun.

Although quilts have always been prized for their texture, adding beads takes quilt texture to a whole new level. Sometimes a handful of beads is all you need to accent a quilt's pieced patchwork or appliquéd landscape scene. The beads add color, sparkle, and high relief as they bring out the beauty of the quilted composition.

On the other hand, you could use a lot of beads on a quilt to make the beads the main event. Beads can encrust a quilt to the point where little, if any, of the background fabric remains visible. Hundreds of beads could create flowing tresses for an appliquéd female figure or form a dense, glittering background for a quilt that, though small, packs a big visual punch.

Whether you bead a quilt lavishly or sparingly, part of the pleasure is shedding the notion that quilts must be functional. While yesterday's quilts covered beds and kept people warm, today's quilts—especially when they're beaded—are more likely to be works of art. Not surprisingly, many beaded quilts are designed as wall hangings, but they can also take the form of book covers, pillows, stylish purses, unusual cards, totems, and much more. All are unique objects worthy of appreciation.

It's easy to quilt with beads. The beading in this book is accomplished with familiar hand stitches, while the quilt making and finishing steps take advantage of contemporary shortcuts such as rotary cutting, machine stitching, and fusible construction where appropriate. The projects on the early pages are quick and easy to complete. The projects that follow are more elaborate and take somewhat more time.

If this is your first experience beading a quilt, you might want to select a project near the front of the book, but this is not a rule. Simply start with the project you find most appealing, and enjoy the rewards of quilting with beads.

Beads

You can find beads in craft stores, quilting shops, and the notions departments of fabric retailers. For

figure 1

a wider selection, there are retail shops, mail order companies, and Internet-based sources that specialize in selling beads and beading supplies. In many regions there are consumer bead shows where vendors offer just about anything a bead enthusiast might desire.

If you're interested in vintage beads, flea markets and estate sales can prove fruitful. You may be able to purchase costume jewelry at a bargain price, then take apart the jewelry at home to harvest some interesting beads.

You can also invent your own beads. Theoretically, anything with a hole can become a bead. A trip to the hardware store, for example, will reveal there are countless nuts, metal washers, and other household items that could be repurposed as beads on a quilt (see figure 1). With a hobby drill, you could pierce a seashell, pottery shard, or little trinket and turn it into a very unique bead. Do-it-yourself beads can also be made from air-dry modeling clay, fused tubes of fabric, and other imaginative materials.

Sew-through buttons have holes, so they're bead candidates, too. For example, an assortment of tiny, mother-of-pearl shirt buttons can add style to a design created from mixed beads, or a larger glass button could act as a focal bead on a quilt.

It's natural to become smitten with beads and beadlike findings. Feel free to follow your impulses and explore the possibilities.

Purchasing Beads

Beads are a globally produced commodity, and the way in which they're sold is not standardized. This is something to keep in mind as you assemble the materials for a beaded quilt.

In general, large, novel beads—the type you might select for the focal point of a design—are sold singly. Small, plain beads—the kind you might select to fill in the background around a focal bead or to make a small-scale design—are often sold in packets containing a limited number of matched beads or a "soup" consisting of assorted plain and fancy beads from one color family. Larger quantities of small beads might be sold in clear vials, strung on hanks, or scooped from a bin and sold by weight.

The materials list for each project will help you estimate the quantity of beads needed to duplicate the design shown in the photograph. With this information, you can obtain the correct number of beads regardless of the way they're sold. If you prefer to substitute beads you've dreamed up on your own or another type of bead that's caught your fancy, you may need a different quantity to complete the project. A good way to be sure you have enough beads for the purpose is to spill them into a saucer or plate, corral them so they're touching, and measure the area they cover. Compare this to the area you expect to cover on the quilt, and purchase or create more beads if necessary.

Actually, it's smart to have more beads than you need. If a bead cracks or breaks, has rough edges, or has a faulty hole, you'll be covered. Chances are any leftover beads will come in handy for future projects.

figure 2

Creating
WITH
Seed Beads

Seed beads are as versatile as they are basic. You can make a finely
detailed design from seed beads alone (see figure 2), using them as fillers
around bigger beads and as companion beads when attaching elements
such as sequins (see figure 3). You can also thread them onto floss to
accent embroidery stitches (see figure 4).

Variations of seed beads include charlottes, which have one facet, and
triangular or hexagonal shapes. Rondelles are flat beads with a center
hole, and they may
have a plain or fancy
surface. The term
rocaille, as used in
this book, refers to
transparent glass seed
beads, sometimes lined
with metallic silver or
gold for extra flourish.
These variations create
textures different from
the classic opaque,
rounded shape and can
add great interest to
a quilt.

figure 3

figure 4

Basic Kinds of Beads

Among the countless types of beads available, two basic kinds—seed beads and bugle beads—are used frequently for the quilts in this book.

SEED BEADS

Classic seed beads are small, plain, rounded beads. They're inexpensive and available in many colors, finishes, and sizes.

Seed bead sizes are usually measured in "aughts," with 0/0 (or 0°) theoretically signifying the largest size and 24/0 the smallest; in fact, probably the largest bead size you'll encounter is 3/0. Most of the projects in this book call for seed beads in the common sizes of 10/0, 11/0, and 12/0. These sizes, which are somewhat interchangeable, are easy to work with and have a good scale for quilted backgrounds.

BUGLE BEADS

Bugle beads are tubes ranging in length from about 1/8 inch (3 mm) to almost 2 inches (5 cm). The longer the bugle bead, the larger its diameter. Usually the diameter of the shorter beads is sized to correspond, more or less, to size 11/0 seed beads. There's a good reason for this. The ends of a bugle bead are sharp and can damage thread. By sewing a round seed bead at each end, you protect the thread as it enters and exits the bugle bead (see figure 5).

Beading Tools & Supplies

You'll need certain kinds of needles and threads to sew beads on quilts.

Needles

Needles for beading must be small enough to pass through the bead's hole. Packaged assortments of hand sewing needles usually contain at least a few needles that will work with the beads you have on hand. For sewing beads on fabric, general-purpose needles called sharps in a size from 7 to 11—whatever size fits through the beads and is comfortable for you to work with—can be used on most of the projects. These needles are sturdy enough to pass through the multiple textile layers that make up a quilt.

Special beading needles, which are long, flexible, and have a very slender eye, are helpful when you must string a number of small beads at once or have to pass the needle through the bead holes a second time to complete a stitch. Beading needles come in various sizes and are available in packaged assortments; like other needles, the higher the number, the smaller the size. In general, you will find a size 10 or 11 helpful for the bead sizes used in this book.

An embroidery needle with a large eye is used for decorative stitches sewn with floss, and sometimes beads are added as you embroider the stitches. When threading beads onto floss, a crewel embroidery needle works well. A crewel needle has an eye that is long and slender in shape; it is more likely to fit through the hole of a bead than a standard embroidery needle, which has a shorter, wider eye.

figure 5

Threads

Threads for beading must be fine yet strong; for the best-looking results, match the thread color to the bead, not the quilt fabric. On a quilt that is lightly beaded and therefore puts minimal weight or strain on the beading thread, regular cotton/polyester or all-polyester sewing thread doubled through the needle works well.

For more extensive beading, you'll need stronger thread. You can choose one of the special beading threads made from nylon or another durable synthetic fiber. Some beading threads come in a selection of sizes ranging from very fine to quite thick; a medium size, sometimes labeled size D, works well for the projects in this book.

Other Beading Tools

You will find a wire needle threader helpful for threading a fine beading needle or for coaxing several strands of embroidery floss through a slender needle eye.

A synthetic polymer conditioner, developed especially for beadwork and packaged in a small plastic cube, can be used to coat thread so it won't tangle or knot as you sew beads in place. Another option for coating thread is beeswax.

A piece of flannel or synthetic suede fabric, used to line a plate or box lid, can be helpful. You can pour beads onto the fabric, and the napped fabric surface will help control the beads as you pick them up on the needle.

Quilt Materials

Most quilts consist of two rectangular panels of cloth—the quilt top and the backing—with a soft batting sandwiched in between. These three textile layers are stacked, basted together temporarily with safety pins, then joined together permanently with hand- or machine-quilted stitches (or a combination of both). The raw edges are usually finished with a binding.

Few projects in this book require large amounts of fabric. Often the fabrics required will be an assortment of small pieces of various prints and colors. You may have on hand what you need if your habit is to save the scraps left over from past sewing projects.

If you prefer to purchase fabrics, you may find it's practical to purchase fat quarters. A fat quarter is a half-yard (.5 m) length of fabric that has been cut in half crosswise to form two fat quarters. For example, if the fabric is 44 inches (111.8 cm) wide, a fat quarter measures 22 x 18 inches (55.9 x 45.7 cm). This may be a more useful amount of fabric for a project than a standard 1/4-yard (.2 m) cut, which would measure 44 x 9 inches (111.8 x 22.9 cm).

Similarly, there are fat eighths and fat halfs available. A fat eighth in the width mentioned above would measure 22 x 9 inches (55.9 x 22.9 cm), and a fat half, 22 x 36 inches (55.9 x 91.4 cm).

The Quilt Top and Backing

The quilt top carries the design. Sometimes the quilt top is backed with interfacing or another stabilizer to help support beaded embellishments.

Each project in this book furnishes a list of the fabrics, beads, and other materials you'll need to duplicate the quilt design that you see in the photograph. If you prefer to use the design as the starting point for an original interpretation, feel free to substitute your own choice of materials. You can use the amounts given as a shopping guide, adjusting the estimates accordingly. For example, if you decide to make a quilt larger than the project sample, you'll need to purchase a greater amount of fabric and other materials.

The backing is usually plain cloth in a solid color or print that relates to the quilt top's design. If you prefer, this layer can be pieced or otherwise embellished to add design interest.

For a beaded quilt, a layer of muslin or other plain fabric is often used as a construction backing. The stitches used to apply the beads are sewn through this layer. The finished backing, which is added when it's time to sew the quilting stitches, covers the construction backing and conceals the beading stitches and knots.

The Batting

Loft refers to the thickness of batting. A low-loft batting is suggested for the quilts in this book because all the designers who used batting chose this type.

Low-loft batting may be made from pure cotton, cotton/synthetic blends, all-polyester fibers, or a polymer-resin fiber derived from corn. This type of fairly flat, thin batting is easy to stitch through, and it's not too bulky to maneuver through a typical household sewing machine. Some low-loft battings are needle punched, glazed, or otherwise processed to make them very stable, and this allows you to quilt as sparingly or as densely as you like. It also provides a firm foundation for supporting beads.

Avoid loosely constructed battings, which are less stable. They probably require close quilting to prevent the batting from shifting and bunching, and this may not work with the beaded design. Chances are these battings would sag under the weight of beaded embellishments, too. Puffy, high-loft battings will bury beads in a deep texture after you quilt them, so they are not suitable for the projects in this book.

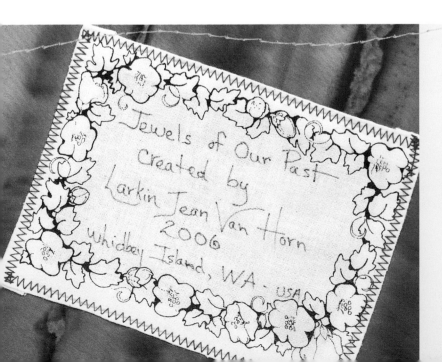

Sign YOUR Quilt

Like any one-of-a-kind creation, the quilt you sew should be signed. Make a label to sew onto the backing that includes your name, the quilt title, the date, and any other information you'd like to record (see figure 6). Write on the label with a fine-tip permanent ink pen, use free-motion stitching (see page 18), or use programmable embroidery lettering if available on your sewing machine. You can also write directly onto the quilt if you prefer.

figure 6

Basic Quilt Tools & Supplies

If you have some sewing experience, you probably have most of the gear you'll need to create beaded quilts. You should have the majority of these items on hand to create any of the projects in this book.

Sewing

A sewing machine that makes a straight and a zig-zag stitch is necessary for making the projects in this book. Newer models may have helpful features such as needle stop up/down, changeable needle positioning, and programmable stitch patterns. These are nice to have but not essential.

If your model has a built-in even-feed feature that moves the top layer of fabric in harmony with the bottom layer, it will give you an advantage when ma-

chine quilting; otherwise you can purchase an accessory called a walking foot (see figure 7), and attach it to the machine for this purpose. For free-motion quilting, you'll need a darning foot (see page 18); usually this accessory is included but it can also be purchased separately. A quilt bar attachment (see page 17) makes it easy to stitch parallel rows without the extra step of marking the quilt; this may be included in the sewing machine's accessory kit or purchased separately.

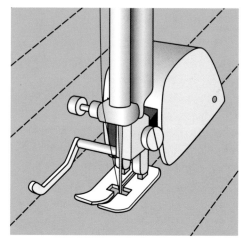

figure 7

Most quilts call for some hand sewing, and for this you'll need a needle and thimble. Sharps, the needles you need for beading, will work well.

For basting quilts, you'll need rustproof safety pins. Good, all-purpose choices are pins in the 1 to 2-inch (2.5 to 5 cm) size range.

Of course, you'll also need thread. Regular cotton/polyester or all-polyester sewing thread, also called all-purpose thread, works well for the quilts on these pages. This type of thread is widely available in a large selection of colors, so you'll find it easy to purchase what you need for a specific project.

Cutting

In addition to common cutting tools such as small scissors and larger shears, a rotary cutting system saves so much time and effort that it belongs in the must-have category. The system requires three tools—the rotary cutter, a clear plastic ruler, and a mat.

The mat and ruler are printed with a measuring grid calibrated in $1/4$-inch (6 mm) measurements. You can place fabric on the mat, align the ruler and mat grids, and roll the cutting blade along the ruler's edge to measure and cut the fabric in one motion. There's no need to measure or mark the fabric beforehand.

For example, cutting narrow crosswise strips for bindings is a common step when making quilts, and rotary cutting makes this quick and easy. To begin, understand that "lengthwise" is parallel to the selvages, while "crosswise" is at right angles to the selvages (see figure 8). Fold the fabric in half lengthwise two times—this folds the fabric into quarters—to prepare for cutting crosswise strips (see figure 9). To cut the fabric into strips, align the bottom edges of the folded fabric with the mat's grid, lay the ruler over the fabric so the ruler's grid aligns with the mat's grid, and cut the strips with the rotary cutter (see figure 10). You'll find a rotary cutter easily slices through multiple fabric layers in a single pass.

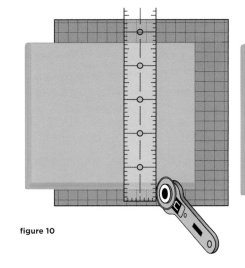

figure 10

There are many sizes of cutters, rulers, and mats, and you may want to collect several of each over time. In general, you will need a cutter in the 45 mm or smaller 28 mm size, a 24 x 6-inch (61 x 15.2 cm) ruler, and a 24 x 18-inch (61 x 45.7 cm) mat. These tools will accommodate any of the binding strips or pieced blocks called for in this book. When a special ruler will streamline a specific quilt project, that ruler will be described in the list of tools.

Pressing

You'll need an iron and ironing board for pressing at almost every stage of making a quilt. Choose an iron you can use with or without steam, depending on the requirements of the supplies you are using.

A portable padded pressing board is helpful when pressing partially completed quilts with the beaded side down. The padded board will cushion the beads to help you avoid dimples and other imprints on the quilt.

lengthwise

crosswise

figure 8

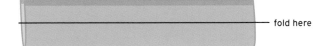

fold here

figure 9

Other Tools & Supplies

For some quilt projects in this book, you'll need additional items.

Freezer paper, a common household product, is useful for making quilt patterns. One side of the paper has a matte finish, while the other is shiny. The paper is transparent enough to allow you to see a template outline so you can trace it directly onto the matte side; you can use a dry iron to press the paper shiny side down onto fabric for a temporary hold.

Parchment paper, another household product, is a heat-resistant, silicone-coated paper normally used for baking. During quilt making, it is used as a nonstick pressing sheet, especially when working with fusible products.

Fusible web, one of those products for which parchment paper is useful, streamlines the steps for making appliqués (see page 18). There are two main web types. Paper-backed fusible web, a classic sewing supply, is a two-ply material that feels rough on the fusible side and smooth on the paper side. The paper is transparent enough to allow you to see a template outline so you can trace it directly on the paper. Follow the manufacturer's directions to apply paper-backed fusible web.

A newer, lightweight fusible web has no paper backing. It was developed for quilters who enjoy combining different types of fabric in their work, so this web works with a wide variety of textiles. It fuses fabrics without making them stiff. It is used along with freezer paper patterns and a parchment paper pressing sheet to make appliqués. Follow the manufacturer's directions to apply lightweight fusible web.

To mark temporary quilting or beading guidelines on a quilt, use a chalk marker or an evaporating ink marker that is designed especially for use on fabrics. For a more durable mark, you can use a pencil or a fine-tip pen with permanent ink; use these marking tools only when the marks will be completely covered by beads or other details in the finished quilt.

Machine Sewing Techniques
Seams

For quilt seams, generally you'll use a $1/4$-inch (6 mm) seam allowance. Practice with scrap fabric to find the best way to sew this narrow seam accurately on your sewing machine.

On some machine models, the throat plate will be etched with a line you can use to guide the raw edge of the fabric the correct distance from the needle. Perhaps the outside edge of the presser foot can be used to align the fabric. If your machine allows you to change the needle position, move the needle to the left or to the right to find a setting that helps you use the throat plate line or the presser foot edge to sew the seam. If necessary, you can always mark the throat plate temporarily with a strip of masking tape to make your own $1/4$-inch (6 mm) seam guide.

Usually quilt seams are pressed to one side (see figure 11). This is an easy way to handle the narrow seam allowances, and some experts feel it makes the seam stronger by reducing stress on the stitches. At times the project instructions say to press the seam allowances open; this may be necessary to reduce bulk because of the fabrics selected or if the design causes seams to fall on top of one another.

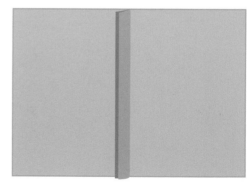

figure 11

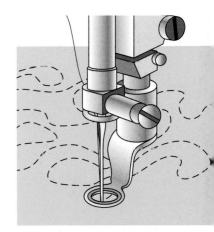

figure 13

Straight-Stitch Quilting

With a few machine adjustments, the same straight stitch you use to sew the quilt seams can be used to quilt the fabric layers together. This method is the most basic form of machine quilting, and it's easy to accomplish when the quilting path follows straight lines.

Prepare the sewing machine by inserting a sharp, new needle. A regular size 75/11 or 80/12 needle works well when using a low-loft batting with lightweight fabrics and regular sewing thread for the quilt top and backing. Select a larger size 90/14 needle when using thicker fabrics or if using the heavier 40 wt. machine embroidery thread. You may need a size 100/16 needle if using 30 wt. machine embroidery thread.

To achieve a balanced stitch that looks the same on the quilt top as on the backing, you may need to loosen the needle tension and lengthen the stitch. Use a scrap sandwich of the quilt top fabric, batting, and backing fabric to test the machine settings until you are satisfied.

To keep all the quilt layers smooth and free of tiny tucks or puckers as you stitch, use a walking foot attachment (see page 14) or engage the even-feed feature (if available on your sewing machine model). Remove the safety pins used to baste the quilt as you approach them; do not stitch over them. You'll find the quilts in this book are small enough to maneuver easily under the needle of the sewing machine.

A quilt bar attachment, added either to a walking foot or a standard presser foot, makes it easy to stitch parallel rows across an entire quilt. Mark and stitch the initial row through the center of the quilt, then let the bar ride on the seam as you stitch a parallel row on one side of it (see figure 12).

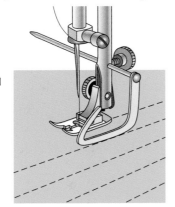

figure 12

Free-Motion Quilting

Most of the quilts in this book call for free-motion quilting. This machine technique takes a little practice to master, but it offers great artistic freedom and does not limit you to stitching in a straight line. That's why many free-motion quilting designs include fluid details such as loops, vines, and swirls (see figure 13).

To set up your sewing machine, follow the directions in the machine manual. Generally, you must remove the regular presser foot and attach a darning foot, which has a small, circular opening through which the needle passes (see figure 14). This foot may also be called a free-motion quilting foot or a darning/embroidery foot. You'll also need to disengage the feed dogs, which are the teeth under the needle that move the fabric; depending on your model, you may have to flick a switch to lower the feed dogs, cover them with a machine accessory, or set the stitch length to "0."

With these two adjustments, you have set up the machine so the needle sews without the machine moving the fabric. Instead, you control the movement of the fabric by spreading out your fingers and placing a hand on each side of the needle (see figure 15). In this position, you can control the stitch length by moving the quilt layers as quickly or as slowly as desired, and you can move them in any direction to create the design you envision.

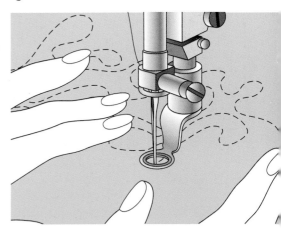

figure 14

figure 15

Fusible Appliqué

Appliqué means cutting out a decorative shape from one fabric and applying it to another fabric. The appliqué methods used for the quilts in this book are especially easy, thanks to fusible products and machine-sewing techniques. You will need to purchase either lightweight fusible web or paper-backed fusible web (see page 16). Follow the project directions to leave the appliqué edges raw or to finish them with hand or machine stitching.

To use lightweight fusible web, trace the appliqué pattern onto the matte side of freezer paper. Stack the freezer paper pattern, matte side up, the fabric, right side up, and the web. Place the stacked layers between sheets of parchment paper (see figure 16). Use an iron to lightly bond the layers together. Let cool. Remove the parchment paper. Use the freezer paper pattern to cut the appliqué from the web-backed fabric (see figure 17), then remove the pattern. Follow the manufacturer's directions to fuse the appliqué on the quilt top.

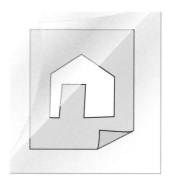

figure 16

figure 17

To use paper-backed fusible web, trace the appliqué pattern onto the paper backing. Note that the final appliqué will be the reverse of this traced pattern. Cut out the tracing roughly, leaving a margin around the outline (see figure 18). Follow the manufacturer's directions to fuse the rough-cut tracing, fusible web side down, onto the wrong side of the fabric. Cut out the appliqué on the traced outline (see figure 19). Peel off the paper backing (see figure 20) to fuse the appliqué to the right side of the quilt top (see figure 21), once again following the manufacturer's directions.

figure 18   **figure 19**

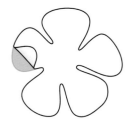

figure 20   **figure 21**

Many projects in this book use heat-sensitive fabrics such as thin synthetics, sheers, and metallics. As you follow the fusible web manufacturer's directions, test the iron setting on fabric scraps to be sure the setting you have selected will not damage the fibers.

Hand Sewing Techniques

Hand sewing is used to apply beads on quilts, for decorative embroidery, and for quilting.

Basic Beading Stitches

For any beading stitch, begin by threading the needle and knotting one end of the thread. If the project instructions say to use a doubled thread, bring the thread ends together and tie them both in the knot. Bring the needle and thread from the back through the quilt top so the knot is on the back (see figure 22). Take a small stitch over the knot for reinforcement.

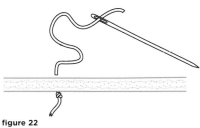

figure 22

To end the beading stitches, take a small stitch for reinforcement, and then knot off by making a thread loop on the back and pulling the needle through the loop two times (see figure 23). Weave the needle through the batting to bring the thread tail out a short distance away (see figure 24), and clip the thread.

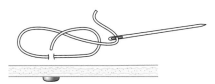

figure 23

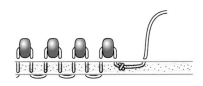

figure 24

A **seed stitch** is used to sew a single bead on the quilt top. A single bead could be used to accent the quilt top, or you can sew a series of single beads in a pattern, either a random one or a regular, repeated pattern. To sew a seed stitch, bring the needle and thread through the quilt top. Pick up one bead on the needle, slide the bead on the thread until it rests on the fabric, then hold the needle perpendicular to the fabric to bring the needle and thread through the quilt top to the backing (see figure 25). After sewing a series of seed stitches, make a knot on the back to secure the stitches before continuing to sew with the same length of thread.

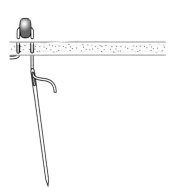

figure 25

A **backstitch** is a secure way to sew a continuous line of beads on the quilt top. Bring the needle and thread through the quilt top. Pick up four to five beads on the needle, slide the beads on the thread until they rest on the fabric, then hold the needle perpendicular to the fabric to bring the needle and thread through the quilt top to the back. Bring the needle and thread through the quilt top at the second-to-last bead. Stitch back through the holes of the last two beads to complete the backstitch (see figure 26).

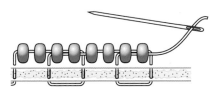

figure 26

A **couching stitch** is used to tack a strand of beads on the quilt top. Bring the needle and thread through the quilt top. Pick up beads with the needle to string them into a strand the length required by the design. At the end of the strand, hold the needle perpendicular to the fabric to bring the thread through the quilt top to the back. Working toward the beginning of the strand, bring the needle and thread through the quilt top about every three to five beads to sew a stitch over the stringing thread (see figure 27).

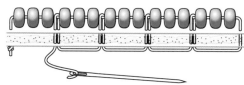

figure 27

To stack beads, thread the beads on the needle, and slide the beads on the thread until they rest on the fabric surface. Skip over the top bead to thread the needle back through the hole of the bead (or beads) underneath (see figure 28).

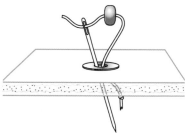

figure 28

Basic Embroidery Stitches

Embroidery adorns a number of quilts in this book. Follow the project instructions to thread an embroidery needle with two to six strands of floss so the stitches look as fine or as bold as the designer intended. For some quilts, beads are slipped onto the embroidery floss as you stitch.

A **buttonhole stitch** often finishes the raw edges of appliqués. The finer the thread, the more closely you can space the stitches. For each buttonhole stitch, take a vertical stitch through the quilt top, bringing the thread under the needle to form a horizontal loop as you stitch (see figure 29).

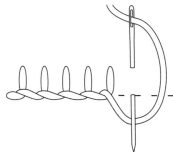

figure 29

Couching is a way to sew a thick, decorative thread or narrow trim on the surface of the quilt top. Thread the needle with a fine thread. Lay the thick thread or narrow trim in place on the quilt top, and overcast it with evenly spaced stitches (see figure 30).

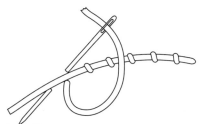

figure 30

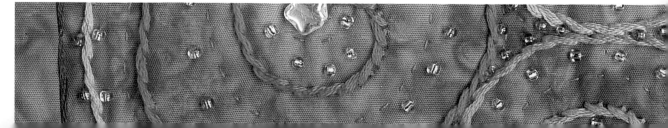

A **cross stitch**, made by sewing two diagonal stitches so they cross in the center (see figure 31), can be embroidered singly for free-style designs. In free-style, the two legs of the cross stitch don't have to match in length.

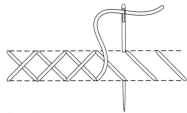

figure 31

A **fly**, or **"Y," stitch** begins at the top left with a loose stitch. A second, vertical stitch secures the center of the loose stitch (see figure 32).

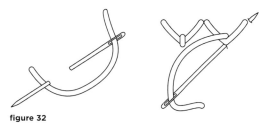

figure 32

A **French knot** is created by wrapping the thread twice around the needle, then inserting the needle back where it came up through the quilt top (see figure 33).

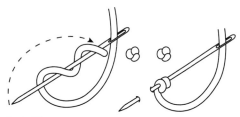

figure 33

A **stem stitch**, often selected to outline a design, is embroidered from left to right (see figure 34).

figure 34

Basic Quilting Stitch

A **running stitch** is used for hand quilting and also for some decorative details. To sew a running stitch, weave the needle in and out of the fabric (see figure 35). Keep the stitches even in length.

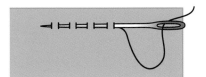

figure 35

At the beginning of a row of running stitches used for quilting, tie a knot at the end of the thread. To hide the knot, insert the needle through the quilt layers so the knot rests on the quilt top. Pull the thread gently from the backing until the knot pops through the top and hides in the batting (see figure 36). Trim the thread tail.

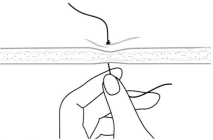

figure 36

At the end of a row of running stitches used for quilting, secure the thread by tying a knot close to the quilt top. Insert the needle through the batting, bringing it out through the quilt top a short distance away. Pull the thread gently until the knot pops through the top (see figure 37). Trim the thread trail.

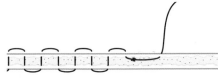

figure 37

QUILT ASSEMBLY TECHNIQUES

Here are the basic steps for assembling your quilt.

Stacking & Basting the Quilt Layers

Prepare to stack the quilt layers by pressing the quilt top and backing to remove any wrinkles. Press a beaded quilt top right side down on a padded pressing surface. Smooth out the batting so it lies flat.

Working on a hard surface large enough to accommodate the quilt, smooth out the backing right side down. Lay the batting on top of the backing, then place the quilt top right side up on the batting (see figure 38). The project instructions usually will tell you to cut the batting larger than the quilt top and the backing larger than the batting; stack the layers so an even margin of batting and backing shows all around the quilt top.

Working from the center of the quilt out toward the edges, baste the layers together with safety pins. Space the pins about 4 to 6 inches (10.2 to 15.2 cm) apart. Check the basted quilt from the back to be sure it's smooth, with no pleats or puckers.

figure 38

Binding the Quilt

A binding is a strip of fabric used to encase the raw edges of the quilt layers. It's usually the final step in making a quilt.

PREPARATION

Prepare the quilt for binding by trimming it evenly so the edges of the quilt top, batting, and backing align. Use a rotary cutter, ruler, and mat to trim the corners at a right angle.

Follow the project instructions to cut fabric strips for the binding. Join them into one long binding strip by overlapping the short ends at right angles with right sides together, then sewing a diagonal seam across the corner; as shown in figure 39, trim the seam allowance to $1/4$ inch (6 mm). Press the seams open to minimize bulk.

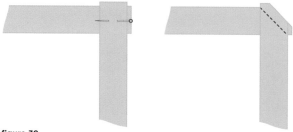

figure 39

STITCHING

With right sides together and working from the quilt top, stitch the binding to the quilt layers with either mitered or butted corners, as stated in the project instructions.

Mitered Corners

Begin applying the binding to the quilt near one corner. Fold the short raw edge on the diagonal $1/4$ inch (6 mm) to the wrong side to start (see figure 40). Using the seam allowance given in the project instructions, begin stitching the binding. At each corner, stop stitching a distance equal to the seam allowance. Take one or two backstitches to lock the seam, clip the threads, and remove the quilt from the sewing machine. Fold the binding straight up so a 45° angle forms in the binding (see figure 41). Fold the binding straight down, and resume stitching (see figure 42).

When you come to the starting point as you near the end of the binding, lap the end of the binding strip over the folded raw edge (see figure 43) to complete stitching the binding seam.

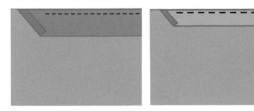

figure 40   figure 41

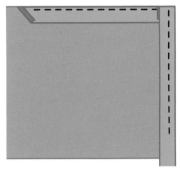

figure 42

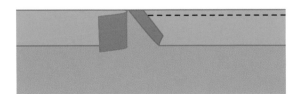

figure 43

Once the binding is stitched around the entire edge of the quilt, fold the binding over the raw edges of all the quilt layers to bring the binding to the quilt backing. Turn under the long raw edge of the binding so the fold just covers the stitches from the binding seam. Work the binding corners with your fingertips to fold a miter—a fold that forms a 45° angle—on the quilt top and on the backing; pin the miters. Slipstitch the folded-under raw

figure 44   figure 45

edge of the binding to the backing by hand (see figure 44), or stitch in the ditch of the binding seam by machine, working from the quilt top (see figure 45).

Butted Corners

Stitch the binding to the top and the bottom edges of the quilt, using the seam allowances given in the project directions. Trim the binding even with the side edges of the quilt. Fold the binding over the raw edges of the quilt layers to the backing. Turn under the raw edge of the binding so the folded edge just covers the stitches from the binding seam. Slipstitch the fold to the backing by hand (see figure 45) or stitch in the ditch of the binding seam by machine, working from the quilt top (see figure 45).

In the same way, stitch the binding to each of the side edges of the quilt, but trim the binding so it is $1/4$ inch (6 mm) longer than the edges of the quilt to allow you to fold under the binding's raw edges at the ends (see figure 46). As when binding the shorter edges, turn under the long raw edge of the binding, and slipstitch the fold or stitch in the ditch. Slipstitch the ends of the binding closed.

figure 46

HANGING AN ART QUILT

To mount an art quilt on the wall, use plastic rings, a fabric sleeve, or a wooden stretcher frame.

Plastic Rings

Two $3/4$-inch (1.9 cm) plastic rings will support a small, lightweight quilt. Sew a ring with a few hand stitches to each upper corner of the backing. Install a pair of small nails, hooks, or screws on the wall for the rings.

Fabric Sleeve

A fabric hanging sleeve will support a quilt of virtually any size or weight, and it's the method you'll need to use for a quilt embellished with a large number of beads. A hanging sleeve is a tube of lightweight fabric sewn to the backing in a way that builds some slack into the tube. When you insert a wooden dowel in the sleeve to hang the quilt, the slack accommodates the bulk of the dowel and enables the quilt to hang smoothly.

To sew a sleeve, follow the project instructions to cut a strip of fabric a little shorter than the finished width of the quilt. Fold the short raw ends under $1/4$ inch (6 mm) two times to make a hem, and stitch (see figure 47). Fold the sleeve in half along its length with right sides together, and stitch a $1/4$-inch (6 mm) seam to make the stack sleeve into a tube. Turn the sleeve right side out, centering the seam on one side (see figure 48).

Sew the top edge of the sleeve, seam side down, by hand to the quilt backing. Pin the bottom edge of the sleeve to the quilt backing so some slack forms in the sleeve (see figure 49). Sew the bottom edge of the sleeve by hand to the quilt backing.

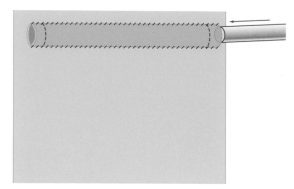

figure 49

Wooden Frame

A wooden stretcher frame can be used to mount a quilt as if it were a painting. Follow the project instructions to make the quilt large enough so there's an equal margin all around the edges to wrap over the sides of the frame to the back. Finish the quilt edges with a short, narrow zigzag stitch.

Lay the quilt right side down on a work surface. Center the frame on the quilt backing so an even margin of the quilt shows all the way around. Use a household staple gun to staple the center top edge of the quilt to the frame. Pull the opposite edge of the quilt taut, and staple the center bottom edge of the quilt to the frame. Staple the center of each side in the same way.

Continue stapling opposite sides, working from the center out each time. After each side has been stapled almost to the corners, fold the corners neatly, and then staple them.

Now that you're familiar with the basic materials, tools, and techniques, it's time to start sewing. You're ready to enjoy the creative rewards of quilting with beads, and take your quilts to a whole new level of achievement.

figure 47

figure 48

the
PROJECTS

By the *sea*

For this scenic quilt, select fabrics with dappled colors to evoke sky, sand, and water. Assorted beads and novelty yarns make a lively mix of colors and textures where the waves deposit seaweed and shells at the shoreline.

DESIGNER:
KATHY DANIELS

FINISHED SIZE:
approximately 10¼ x 9¼ inches
(26 x 23.5 cm)

Materials

Quilt top:
Medium blue cotton fabric, 13 x 6 inches (33 x 15.2 cm)
Blue/green cotton fabric, 13 x 6 inches (33 x 15.2 cm)
Golden tan cotton fabric, 3 x 13 inches (7.6 x 33 cm)
Small scraps of blue and blue/green fabrics
Turquoise blue nylon net, 3 inches (7.6 cm) square

Beads:
About 100 to 150 assorted small blue and green beads
About 50 to 75 assorted small white beads
Several small shells

Batting:
Low-loft batting, 13 x 11 inches (33 x 27.9 cm)

Backing:
Blue cotton fabric, 13 x 11 inches (33 x 27.9 cm)

Binding:
Coordinating cotton fabric, 4 x 12 inches (10.2 cm x 30.5 cm)
Paper-backed fusible web, 4 x 12 inches (10.2 cm x 30.5 cm)

Thread, etc:
Clear monofilament nylon thread
Blue and gold sewing thread
About five 12-inch (30.5 cm) pieces of blue and green
   novelty yarns
Gold metallic sewing thread
Two ¾-inch (1.9 cm) plastic rings

Tools & Supplies

Hand-sewing needle
Beading needle
Jewelry glue

Instructions

1 Lay the medium blue fabric on the batting to represent the sky. Cut three curves along one long edge of the tan fabric to represent the sand. Overlap the sand fabric over the sky about ⅛ inch (3 mm), then overlap the blue/green fabric representing the water over the sand about ⅛ inch (3 mm). Add small pieces of blue and blue/green fabrics to the sky and water areas as desired to complete the quilt top.

2 Adjust the sewing machine for straight stitching. Fill the bobbin with blue thread. Thread the needle with matching thread to stitch along the raw edge of each fabric section. Trim the quilt top roughly even with the edges of the batting.

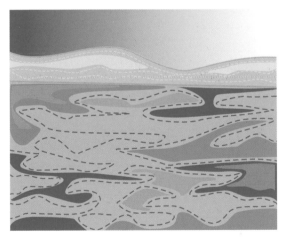

figure 1

3 Adjust the sewing machine for free-motion quilting. Thread the needle with matching thread to stitch curving rows in the sand area and a pattern of waves in the water area (see figure 1).

DESIGNER *Note:* As a creative option to add interest to the "water" fabric, you could apply turquoise, blue, and violet fabric paints with light brushstrokes. For highlights, brush gold fabric paint on a small piece of bubble wrap packing material and stamp the fabric.

4 Thread the hand-sewing needle with blue thread. Use a running stitch to quilt several curving rows in the sky area to represent clouds.

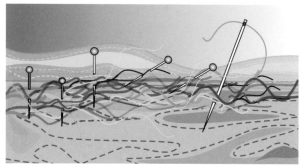

figure 2

5 Arrange the novelty yarns along the top of the water to represent seaweed. Pin the yarns in place. Tack the yarns about every inch (2.5 cm) with hand stitches (see figure 2).

6 Thread the beading needle with blue thread. Sew blue and green beads clustered very closely together in two places along the quilted waves. Sew some beads among the novelty yarns as accents. Place all beads about 2 inches (5 cm) in from the edges of the quilt.

7 Trim the nylon net into an irregular wave shape. Pin it to the water area where more detail is needed. Thread the hand-sewing needle with metallic thread. Apply the net to the quilt top with a series of free-form cross stitches.

8 Thread the beading needle with nylon thread. Sew clusters of white beads above the sand to represent foam.

9 Lay the backing right side down. Stack the quilt top/batting right side up on the backing. Baste the layers together with a few safety pins. Trim the quilt to $10^{1}/_{4}$ x $9^{1}/_{4}$ inches (26 x 23.5 cm).

10 Follow the manufacturer's directions to apply fusible web to the binding fabric. Cut four $^{3}/_{4}$ x 12-inch (1,9 x 30.5 cm) binding strips.

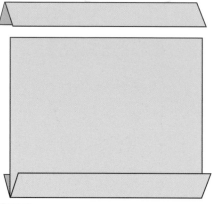

figure 3

figure 4

11 Trim a binding strip to fit each top and bottom edge of the quilt. Remove the paper backing. Fold each strip in half along its length, web sides together, and crease the fold with your fingers. Fuse the binding to the top and bottom edges, folding each strip over the raw edges of the layers to encase them (see figure 3). Fold each end of the two remaining binding strips at a 45° angle to look like a miter (see figure 4), and fuse the binding strips to the side edges.

12 Adjust the sewing machine for a decorative or a straight stitch. Stitch along the inner edge of the binding through all layers around the quilt.

13 Glue the shells to the seaweed.

14 Sew the rings to the upper corners of the backing.

Flower
MAGNETS

Choose from among the mix-and-match templates to make a
bouquet of magnets from bits and pieces of fabric, metallic threads,
beads, and assorted findings. The delightful embellishments turn
each blossom into a miniature work of art.

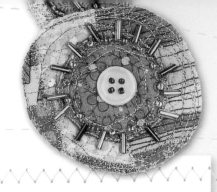
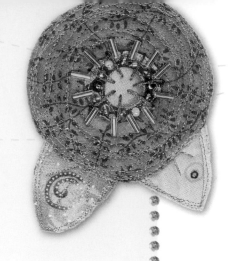

DESIGNER:
MARJORIE DADE LUCAS KAFADER

FINISHED SIZE:
Approximately 2½ x 3½ inches
(6.4 x 8.9 cm)

Materials (for one magnet)

Magnet top:
Three contrasting 5-inch (12.7 cm) squares of cotton print fabric
Paper-backed fusible web, 5 x 15 inches (12.7 x 38.1 cm)

Batting:
Three 5-inch (12.7 cm) squares of synthetic fleece in colors
    that blend with the cotton fabrics

Beads:
About 20 small bugle beads in assorted colors and sizes
About 20 seed beads in assorted colors and sizes
½-inch (1.3 cm) bead, button, or jewelry finding

Backing:
Stiff nonwoven fusible interfacing, 5 inches (12.7 cm) square

Thread, etc:
Assorted colors of metallic machine embroidery thread
Neutral color of machine bobbin thread
Assorted colors of nylon beading thread, size D
Circular ceramic magnet, 1 inch (2.5 cm) in diameter

Tools & Supplies

Pencil
Sewing machine needle for metallic thread
Beading needle
Glue gun and glue

Templates

See page 118

Instructions

1 Choose one flower, flower center, and leaf template. Trace the templates onto the paper backing of the fusible web. As if making appliqués, follow the manufacturer's directions to apply the web to the cotton fabric squares. Cut out the magnet sections.

2 Peel off the paper backing from each magnet section. Fuse each section to a color-coordinated square of synthetic fleece. Do not cut out the sections at this time.

3 Insert the needle for metallic thread in the sewing machine. Adjust the machine for straight-stitch quilting. Select a very short stitch length of about 20 per inch (2.5 cm). Thread the needle with metallic thread. Fill the bobbin with bobbin thread. Beginning at the edge and working toward the center, stitch three to four irregular circles on the flower section and two to three similar circles on the flower center section. Thread a second metallic thread through the needle, and repeat. Thread a third metallic thread through the needle, and repeat.

DESIGNER *Note:* The nonwoven interfacing used to back each magnet doubles as a label. Use a fine-tip marker with permanent ink to sign your name and write the date directly on the interfacing.

By sewing on a pin instead of gluing on a magnet, these flowers can be made into a pin for a lapel or hat. Then you can wear your masterpiece whenever you need a splash of color.
— MARJORIE DADE LUCAS KAFADER, DESIGNER

4 Thread a fourth metallic thread through the sewing machine needle. Stitch around the edge of the leaf section, then stitch irregular triangles on the leaf. Repeat if desired, changing the metallic thread color each time.

5 Cut out the magnet sections.

6 Pin the flower center on the flower. Thread the beading needle with beading thread. Sew seed beads around the edge of the flower center, sewing the stitches through all the fabric layers. Sew a large bead, button, jewelry finding, or sequins to the center as a focal point. Add bugle and seed beads as desired around the focal point.

7 Sew one or more rows of bugle beads alternating with seed beads as a center vein on the leaf.

8 Arrange the flower so it overlaps the leaf slightly. Sew the leaf to the wrong side of the flower with small hand stitches.

9 Press the completed flower, right side down.

10 Place the stiff interfacing, fusible side down, on the wrong side of the magnet. Follow the manufacturer's directions to fuse the interfacing to the magnet. Trim the excess interfacing around the edge of the magnet.

11 Glue the ceramic magnet to the center of the completed flower on the interfacing side.

DESIGNER Note: To make the most interesting magnet, use a wide variety of fabrics, beads, and decorative machine embroidery threads. For the focal point at the center of the flower, you can use part of a piece of costume jewelry, a colorful button, some sequins, or a sparkling bead. Three leaf templates are provided, and you can use one or two per magnet as desired.

hugs & kisses
CARD

Why send hugs and kisses in a low-key style when you can transmit your sentiments with lavish embellishments? This mixed-media love note features a heart made from a lace flower, a metal button, and hundreds of mixed beads.

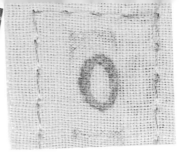
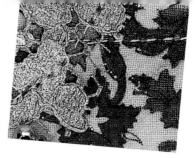

DESIGNER:
MAVIS LEAHY

FINISHED SIZE:
approximately 7 x 5 inches
(17.8 x 12.7 cm)

Materials

Card front:
White muslin fabric, 1 x 2 ½-inch (2.5 X 6.4 cm) strip
Brown lace, 3 x 5 inches (7.6 x 12.7 cm)
Floral print fabric, 4½ x 3½ inches (11.4 x 8.9 cm)
Lace flower, about 1 inch (2.5 cm) in diameter
5 inches (12.7 cm) of embroidered ribbon, 1 inch
   (2.5 cm) wide
Card-weight handmade paper, 7 x 5-inch piece
   (17.8 x 12.7 cm)

Beads:
About 300 size 10/0 assorted beads
Metal button, about ⅝ inch (1.6 cm) in diameter

Thread, etc:
Yellow/gold rayon machine embroidery thread
Off-white sewing thread
Envelope, 5¼ x 7¼ inches (13.3 x 18.4 cm)

Tools & Supplies

Yellow/orange and metallic gold fabric paint
Small paintbrush
X and O rubber stamps
Stamp pad with permanent ink
Tracing paper
Pencil
Fabric marker with evaporating ink
Beading needle
Glue stick

Template

See page 118

Instructions

1 Use the paintbrush to apply yellow/orange paint to the muslin strip. Apply gold paint to the lace. Let the paint dry. Stamp a row of X and O letters on the strip.

2 Trace the heart template, and cut it out. Pin the template to the center of the floral fabric on the right side. Trace around the template with the fabric marker.

3 Thread the beading needle with rayon thread. Sew a row of beads on the traced heart outline. Sew the lace flower in the center of the heart and the button in the center of the flower. Fill in the remaining area of the heart with beads.

4 Arrange the lace, ribbon, beaded heart, and muslin strip on the handmade paper. Use a small amount of glue to baste the embellishments in place.

5 Adjust the sewing machine for straight stitching. Select a long stitch, about seven per inch (2.5 cm). Thread the needle with rayon thread. Fill the bobbin with off-white thread. Stitch around the edge of each fabric, lace, and ribbon embellishment. At the end of a row of stitches, do not backstitch because this will weaken the paper; simply trim the thread ends.

6 Sew a row of beads below the muslin strip.

7 Insert the card into the envelope.

" I love creating projects with treasured scraps of vintage and antique fabrics and findings, such as a small piece of embroidered silk, salvaged from a shattered crazy quilt from the late 1800s. It is the challenge I enjoy. "
– MAVIS LEAHY, DESIGNER

Latin
BEAUTY

Blend subject and style, the old and the new, to create this small
quilt. Inspired by folk art retablos, the design features devotional
charms, game board images framed in bottle caps, jewelry fragments,
and colorful beads.

DESIGNER:
HEATHER NOBLITT

FINISHED SIZE:
approximately 9½ x 7 inches
(24.1 x 17.8 cm)

Materials

Quilt top and backing:

Pink batik cotton fabric, one piece 8½ x 5½ inches
(21.6 x 14 cm) and two pieces 9 x 6½ inches (22.9 x 16.5 cm)
Firm nonwoven interfacing, 8¾ x 6¼ inches (22.2 x 15.9 cm)
Pink lace fabric, 9½ x 7 inches (24.1 x 17.8 cm)
Vintage pink cotton fabric, 6 x 6½ inches (15.2 x 16.5 cm)
Blue cotton fabric, 4 x 3½ inches (10.2 cm x 8.9 cm)
Face image printed on ink-jet fabric
½ yard (.5 m) of paper-backed fusible web, 20 inches
(50.8 cm) wide
Orange rickrack, 7 inches (17.8 cm)
Pink lace hem tape, 15 inches (38.1 cm)

Beads:

About 400 size 11/0 pearl seed beads
About one hundred ¼-inch (6 mm) red bugle beads
About 72 size 11/0 pink seed beads
About 60 small round pink sequins
About twelve 5 mm (⁵⁄₃₂ inch) flower sequins in assorted colors
Two milagros religious charms
Vintage jewelry fragments
Five small red ribbon roses
Three metal bottle caps
Loteria game card

Thread, etc:

9 inches (22.9 cm) of pink ribbon, ¼ inch (6 mm) wide
Pink sewing thread
Pink nylon beading thread, size D

Tools & Supplies

Pencil
Fabric glue
Quarter coin
Water-based dimensional glue
Small hand-sewing needle for beading
Pinking shears

Templates

See page 118

Instructions

1 Trace the arch templates onto the paper backing of fusible web. Follow the manufacturer's directions to apply the fusible web to the vintage fabric for the large arch appliqué and the blue fabric for the small arch appliqué. Cut out the appliqués.

2 Follow the manufacturer's directions to apply fusible web to the wrong side of the face image. Cut out the face image appliqué.

3 Arrange the arch and face image appliqués on the smaller piece of pink batik fabric. Fuse the appliqués.

4 With right sides up, stack one of the larger pink batik pieces, the pink lace fabric, and the appliquéd pink fabric. An even margin of lace should show all around the appliquéd pink fabric. Adjust the sewing machine to sew a zigzag stitch. Thread the needle and fill the bobbin with pink thread. Stitch through all layers around the edge to make the quilt top.

5 Use fabric glue to apply the quilt top to the interfacing. Let the glue dry.

6 Use fabric glue to apply rows of lace tape and rickrack to the quilt top above the arches. Let the glue dry.

7 Use a quarter coin as a pattern to cut three images from the game card. Glue one image inside each bottle cap with dimensional glue. Let the glue dry.

8 Thread the needle with beading thread. Use a backstitch to sew bugle beads with a seed bead at each end in a row outlining each arch and the side and bottom edges of the quilt top. In the same way, use bugle and seed beads to create the halo over the face image, but arrange the bugle beads like radiating spokes. Stack a seed bead and flower sequin, and sew each stack individually near the top of the quilt. Stack a seed bead and round sequin, and sew each stack individually to fill open areas on the quilt.

9 Use fabric glue to apply the bottle caps, vintage jewelry fragments, ribbon roses, and milagros to the quilt top. Glue the ends of the ribbon to the top corners of the interfacing on the wrong side of the quilt top. Let the glue dry.

10 Trim the raw edge of the remaining piece of pink batik fabric with pinking shears. Sew the fabric to the back of the quilt with hand stitches.

" I find working with color schemes and texture helps me build my projects, layer by layer. Adding found elements, such as items you buy at yard sales, is a great way to add uniqueness to any project. **"**
– HEATHER NOBLITT, DESIGNER

TRIPTYCH *Landscape*

  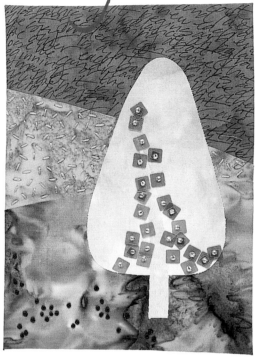

The basis for this three-part art quilt is a landscape created with fusible appliqués, some of which display your handwriting as a design detail. Feel free to combine beads and embroidery stitches in your own way to personalize the composition.

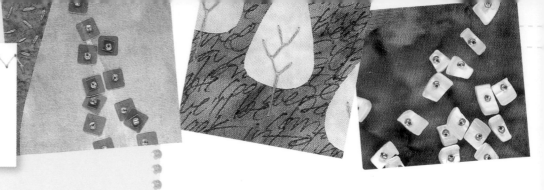

DESIGNER:
DEBORAH BOSCHERT

FINISHED SIZE:
three panels, each 7 x 5 inches (17.8 x 12.7 cm)

Materials

Quilt top and backing:
Blue, lavender, green, and multicolor batik cotton fabrics,
    22 x 10 inches (55.9 x 25.4 cm) of each
Light blue batik cotton fabric, 10 inches (25.4 cm) square
Light purple batik cotton fabric, 6 inches (15.2 cm) square
1½ (1.4 m) yards of lightweight fusible web, 20 inches
    (50.8 cm) wide

Batting:
Low-loft batting, three 7 x 5-inch (17.8 x 12.7 cm) pieces

Beads*:
Forty 4 mm ($^5/_{32}$ inch) square blue sequins
Twenty 7 mm ($^7/_{32}$ inch) square green sequins
90 green seed beads
9 lavender seed beads
30 aqua shell-fragment beads
Bead quantities are approximate

Thread, etc:
Dark green, light green, bright green, gray, blue, and purple
    embroidery floss
Blue, green, and lavender nylon beading thread, size D
Six ¾-inch (1.9 cm) plastic rings

Tools & Supplies

Cardstock with 7 x 5-inch (17.8 x 12.7 cm) opening
Parchment paper
Chalk pencil
Freezer paper
Fine-point pen with permanent black ink
Embroidery needle with a large eye
Beading needle
Damp cloth

Templates

See page 119

Instructions

1 Use the chalk pencil and the opening on the cardstock to mark three 7 x 5-inch (17.8 x 12.7 cm) outlines 1 inch (2.5 cm) apart on a piece of parchment paper.

2 Follow the manufacturer's directions to apply fusible web to the wrong side of the quilt top fabrics.

3 Use the web-backed fabrics to build the appliqué landscape within the chalk-marked outlines. Begin with the sky by covering the upper third of the three outlines with blue fabric. Use the chalk pencil to mark a continuous, curved cutting line for the lavender hill (see figure 1). Trim the sky appliqué ⅛ inch (3 mm) below the cutting line. Press the sky appliqué temporarily on the parchment paper. Since part of the marked outline has now been covered, use the cardstock opening as a template to mark the complete outline. In the same way, mark, cut, and press in place the lavender hill, green hill, and multicolored hill. Use the fabric scraps to cut three 6½ x 4½-inch (16.5 x 11.4 cm) backing pieces, and reserve. Reserve the multicolored scraps to cut the appliqués.

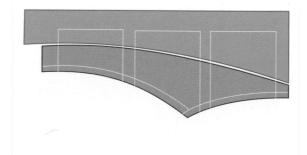

figure 1

4   Trace the house and tree templates onto the matte side of the freezer paper. Press each pattern, shiny side down, on the right side of the fabric to cut each appliqué. Cut the medium house appliqué from a scrap of multicolored fabric. Cut the remaining appliqué houses and trees from the light purple and light blue fabrics.

5   Use the pen to fill in a house, hill, and sky appliqué with your handwriting. Use the content of your choice, such as random words, a journal entry, a poem, or the lyrics from a favorite song.

6   Arrange the house and tree appliqués on the landscape. Fuse the shapes in place following the manufacturer's directions.

7   Peel the entire landscape off the parchment paper. Cut out each 7 x 5-inch (17.8 x 12.7 cm) panel, adding a margin of $1/2$ inch (1.3 cm) extending all around each marked outline (see figure 2). Remove any chalk marks by dabbing with a damp cloth.

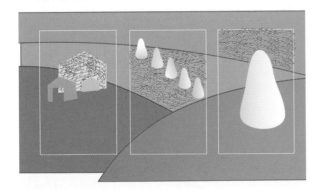

figure 2

8   Place each panel, right side down, on the pressing surface. Place a piece of batting on top of each panel, making sure the panel extends $1/2$ inch (1.3 cm) past the batting all around. Press to fuse each piece of batting to a panel.

9   Thread the embroidery needle with two strands of floss to add embroidery stitches such as fly stitches, French knots, running stitches, cross stitches, and seed stitches to each panel. Use the photograph as a guide for embroidery, or choose stitches you prefer. Change the floss color to contrast with the various landscape areas.

10   Thread the beading needle with green beading thread. Stack a green seed bead on a green sequin, and sew several individual stacks near the trunk of the large tree appliqué. Stack a blue sequin on some of the green sequins before you add the seed bead. In the same way, use blue beading thread to sew the remaining blue sequins and green seed beads among the embroidery stitches. Sew a single shell bead with a green seed bead to the small house appliqué. In the same way, sew the remaining shell beads to the multicolored hill in the center panel.

11   Thread the beading needle with lavender thread. Sew the lavender seed beads on the medium house.

12   Trim the corners of each panel diagonally within the $1/2$-inch (1.3 cm) margin. Fold the $1/2$-inch (1.3 cm) margin over the raw edge to the back of each panel, and fuse to the batting.

13   Place a backing section on each panel to cover the batting and the raw edges of the folded-back margin. Fuse each backing in place.

14   Sew two plastic rings near the upper corners of the backing on each panel.

" I really enjoy the design challenge of making each piece of the triptych an interesting composition of its own, while still making them work together as a whole. "
– DEBORAH BOSCHERT, DESIGNER

chick on the *run*

Whimsical appliqués create this charming scene in a free-form style that's fun and easy to sew. A combination of glass and wooden beads, plus a few buttons, complement the casual composition.

DESIGNER:
CHRISTINA ROMEO

FINISHED SIZE:
approximately 10 inches (25.4 cm) square

Materials

Quilt top:
Off-white cotton fabric, 11 inches (27.9 cm) square

Appliqués:
Circle-print green fabric, 3 x 6 inches (7.6 x 15.2 cm)
Yellow fabric, 8 x 10 inches (20.3 x 25.4 cm)
Olive green fabric, 3 x 5 inches (7.6 x 12.7 cm)
Brown fabric, 2 inches (5 cm) square

Beads:
About 28 small round rust beads
About 16 medium round brown wooden beads
About 45 assorted medium square wooden beads
One medium silver bead
About 10 small green glass beads
Three brown buttons, about ⅝ inch (1.6 cm) in diameter

Backing and Binding:
Medium yellow cotton fabric, 11 x 20 inches (27.9 x 50.8 cm)

Batting:
Low-loft batting, 11 inches (27.9 cm) square

Thread, etc:
Gold and off-white sewing thread
White embroidery floss
Two ¾-inch (1.9 cm) plastic rings

Tools & Supplies

Pencil
Freezer paper
Fabric glue stick
Embroidery needle with a large eye
Small hand-sewing needle for beading

Templates

See page 119

*¼-inch (6 mm) and ½-inch (1.3 cm) seam allowances
as noted*

Instructions

1 Trace the templates onto the matte side of freezer paper to make the appliqué patterns. Cut out the patterns roughly.

2 Place the patterns, shiny side down, on the right side of the following appliqué fabrics: tree and hill, yellow fabric; moon, upper trunk, and one of the chick legs, olive green fabric; chick body, green circle-print fabric; lower trunk and one of the chick legs, brown fabric. Press to hold the patterns temporarily on the fabrics. Cut out each pattern on the traced outline to make the appliqués.

3 Remove the pattern from the tree appliqué. Cut scant ½-inch (1.3 cm) snips into the raw edge. Fold the ½-inch (1.3 cm) seam allowance to the wrong side. Use the glue stick to hold the seam allowance in place.

4 Remove the pattern from the upper and lower trunk sections. Fold the ¼-inch (6 mm) seam allowance to the wrong side, and press.

5 Remove the patterns from the remaining appliqués. Arrange the moon, tree, and hill appliqués on the quilt top. Use the glue stick to hold them in place. Adjust the sewing machine for straight stitching. Thread the needle and fill the bobbin with off-white sewing thread. Stitch around the edges of each of these appliqués two to four times in a free-form style.

"Most of my designs for textile projects start from a simple pencil and paper sketch, brought to life through fabric. I design by instinct, using how I feel as my guide. – CHRISTINA ROMEO, DESIGNER"

6 Arrange the remaining appliqués on the quilt top. Use the glue stick to hold them in place. Stitch around the edge of the chick body twice in a free-form style. Stitch close to the edges of the two trunk sections. Adjust the sewing machine for zigzag stitching. Stitch along the center of each of the chick legs.

7 Thread the embroidery needle with two strands of floss. Stitch a row of cross stitches along the center of each trunk section.

8 Place the quilt top, right side up, on the batting. Baste with safety pins.

9 Thread the small hand-sewing needle with gold thread. Sew the three buttons on the hill. Use a backstitch to sew square wooden beads in a row that curls around the buttons. Use a seed stitch to sew clusters of four round rust beads on the tree as fruit. Use a backstitch to sew a row of round brown wooden beads along the right-hand edge of the tree. Sew the silver bead on the chick for an eye. Use a seed stitch to sew green beads on the moon in a random arrangement.

10 Cut a backing 11 inches (27.9 cm) square and four 2 x 11-inch (5 x 27.9 cm) binding strips from medium yellow fabric.

11 Stack the quilt top, right side up, on the backing, right side down. Baste the layers together with safety pins.

12 Adjust the sewing machine for straight-stitch quilting. Thread the needle and fill the bobbin with off-white sewing thread. Beginning at the top of the moon appliqué, stitch around the moon several times, and then stitch in a continuous line around the chick, hill, and tree appliqués. Thread the needle with gold sewing thread. Stitch around the appliqués a second time in the same way.

13 Trim the quilt so it measures 10 inches (25.4 cm) square. Bind the quilt, using a 1/2-inch (1.3 cm) seam allowance and butted corners. Apply the binding to the side edges first, and then to the top and bottom edges. Topstitch each binding strip along the inner edge and along the outside edge.

14 Sew the rings to the backing to hang the quilt.

Broken
DISHES

Give chipped and broken plates a new purpose by turning them into one-of-a-kind beads. This quilt takes its name not only from the shards used as embellishments, but also from the traditional patchwork design used for the quilt top.

DESIGNER:
KATE GLEZEN CUTKO

FINISHED SIZE:
approximately 12 x 22 inches (30.5 x 55.9 cm)

Materials

Quilt top:
Fat quarters of five or six assorted small-scale print cotton
  fabrics and two large-scale prints

Backing and hanging sleeve:
1/2 yard (.5 m) of print cotton fabric, 44 inches (111.8 cm) wide

Batting:
Low-loft cotton batting, 14 x 24 inches (35.6 x 61 cm)

Binding:
1/8 yard (.1 m) of cotton print fabric, 44 inches (111.8 cm) wide

Beads:
About 16 pottery shards
About 24 assorted buttons, 1/4 to 3/8 inch (6 to 9.5 mm)
  in diameter

Thread, etc:
Sewing thread to match the backing and the buttons
Embroidery floss to match the pottery shards
Clear monofilament nylon thread

Tools & Supplies

4-inch (10.2 cm) square transparent ruler
Rotary drill and drill press
Diamond burr drill bit
Embroidery needle with a large eye
Hand sewing needle
Fray retardant

1/4-inch (6 mm) seam allowance unless noted otherwise

Instructions

1 Cut a 14 x 24-inch (35.6 x 61 cm) backing and a 4 1/2 x 20-inch (11.4 x 50.8 cm) hanging sleeve from the 1/2 yard (.5 m) of fabric.

2 Cut nineteen 5-inch (12.7 cm) squares from the assorted fabrics. Cut each square diagonally from corner to corner to create four triangles.

3 Arrange the triangles into 18 blocks with two matching pairs of triangles in each block. Sew the triangles together to make each block.

4 Use the ruler to trim each block to 4 inches (10.2 cm) square.

5 Arrange the trimmed blocks into six rows of three blocks each. Sew the blocks together for each row. Press the seams in each row to one side, alternating the direction with each row. Sew the rows together. Press the seams in one direction.

6 Stack and baste the quilt layers.

DESIGNER Note: Create pottery shards from broken and chipped plates you have on hand or use inexpensive flea market finds. Wrap the plates in an old towel, wear safety goggles, and break the plates into shards with a hammer. An assortment of sizes ranging from nickel to half dollar works well. Sand any sharp edges. Use the shards to help you select appropriate print fabrics.

7 Adjust the sewing machine for straight-stitch quilting. Thread the needle and fill the bobbin with sewing thread. Stitch a simple wave design of curving rows spaced about 1 inch (2.5 cm) apart.

8 Cut 2-inch-wide (5 cm) strips crosswise from the binding fabric. Bind the quilt, using a $^{1}/_{2}$-inch (1.3 cm) seam allowance and mitered corners.

9 Follow the drill manufacturer's directions to drill two holes in each shard.

10 Arrange the beads and assorted buttons in a curved row to echo the quilted waves. Sew each bead with a double strand of nylon thread or three strands of floss. Tie the thread or floss in a secure knot on the backing. Seal each knot with a drop of fray retardant. Sew each button on the quilt with matching thread.

11 Attach the hanging sleeve.

" If you are inspired by an object, find a way to make it work on your quilt. A drill will put a hole through most things, and if not, wrap the object in fine gauge wire or experiment with an embellishing glue. "
– KATE GLEZEN CUTKO, DESIGNER

FLOWERS ON A *hill*

The border on this pretty quilt frames a garden of yo-yo flowers blooming
with seed beads and touches of silk ribbon embroidery. A scattering of
green bugle beads makes the hillside sparkle like the morning dew.

DESIGNER:
MARNÉ CALES

FINISHED SIZE:
approximately 11 x 13 inches (27.9 x 33 cm)

Materials

Quilt top:
Green print fabric, 6 x 11 inches (15.2 x 27.9 cm)
Light blue print fabric, 6 x 11 inches (15.2 x 27.9 cm)
About six assorted pink floral mini-print fabrics, about
   5 inches (12.7 cm) square
Pale pink floral mini-print fabric, 6 x 12 inches
   (15.2 x 30.5 cm)
Medium pink floral-print fabric, 6 x 12 inches
   (15.2 x 30.5 cm)

Batting:
Low-loft cotton batting, 12 x 14 inches (30.5 x 35.6 cm)

Backing, binding, and hanging sleeve:
Fat quarter of lavender floral-print fabric

Beads:
About 40 pink and 20 green seed beads in assorted sizes
About 180 small green bugle beads

Thread, etc:
Pale pink and green sewing thread
Green, pink, and light blue embroidery floss
About 1/2 yard (.5 m) of pale pink silk ribbon,
   5/32 inch (4 mm) wide
About 1/2 yard (.5 m) of bright pink silk ribbon,
   7/32 inch (7 mm) wide
About 1 yard (.9 m) of green silk ribbon,
   7/32 inch (7 mm) wide

Tools & Supplies

Chalk fabric marker
Embroidery needle with a large eye
Freezer paper
Pencil
Small hand-sewing needle for beading

Templates

See page 120

1/4-inch (6 mm) seam allowance unless noted otherwise

Instructions

1 Use the chalk marker to draw a simple curved
seamline for the hill on the green print fabric.
Mark a cutting line 1/4 inch (6 mm) above the
seamline (see figure 1). Cut out the hill section for
the quilt top.

figure 1

2 Fold under the seam allowance along the top
of the hill section, and press. Lay it right side
up on the right side of the light blue print fabric for
the sky. Pin the hill and sky sections together at the
hill seamline. Trace the seamline onto the sky section,
and mark a cutting line 1/4 inch (6 mm) below (see
figure 2). Cut out the sky section.

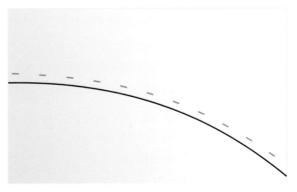

figure 2

3   Sew the hill and sky sections on the seamline with right sides together to make the quilt top. Clip the curved seam allowance where necessary so the fabric lays flat. Press the seam toward the hill. Trim the quilt top to measure 8 x 10 inches (20.3 x 25.4 cm).

4   Thread the embroidery needle with two strands of green floss. Sew a buttonhole stitch along the seam.

5   Cut twelve 2-inch (5 cm) squares from the assorted mini-print fabrics. Reserve the remaining fabrics for the yo-yo circles. Sew two rows of six squares each for the quilt top border. Press the seams of each row in one direction.

6   Cut a 2 x 12-inch (5 x 30.5 cm) strip from the pale pink and medium pink fabrics for the quilt top border. Reserve the remaining fabrics for the yo-yo circles.

7   Sew one pieced border strip to the upper edge of the quilt top. Press the seam away from the center. Sew the other pieced border strip to the right-hand edge of the quilt top, and press in the same way. Sew one 2 x 12-inch border strip to the bottom edge of the quilt top. Trim the strip even with the quilt top on the left-hand side. Press the seam away from the center. In the same way, sew the other 2 x 12-inch (5 x 30.5 cm) border strip to the left-hand side of the quilt top, and press.

8   Use the pencil to trace the yo-yo circle templates onto the matte side of the freezer paper. Trace the larger circle two times and the smaller circle three times. Cut out the freezer paper patterns.

9   Press the patterns, shiny side down, on the reserved pink print fabrics. Cut out the yo-yo circles.

"" This is a great project for using up all those little bits and bobs not only in your scrap pile, but also in your bead box. And I just love yo-yo's; they look like flowers to me. – MARNÉ CALES, DESIGNER ""

10 Thread a needle with pink sewing thread. Double the thread, and knot the ends. To make each yo-yo flower, fold under the raw edge of a fabric circle 1/4 inch (6 mm). Sew running stitches close to the fold. Pull the thread to gather the fabric snugly. Secure the thread with several small stitches, and trim the thread tail.

11 Arrange the yo-yo flowers on the quilt top above the hill section. Sew each flower to the quilt top with small hand stitches.

12 Thread the embroidery needle with three to six strands of green floss or green silk ribbon to sew the flower stems. Sew some of the stems with a stem stitch and some with a row of small, horizontal straight stitches. Couch green silk ribbon for one stem; thread the small needle with green sewing thread to sew a free-style row of green seed beads on this stem.

13 Thread the embroidery needle with pink silk ribbon to sew lazy daisy stitches as petals around two of the flowers (see figure 3). Thread the small needle with pink sewing thread to sew seed beads as desired around some of the flowers.

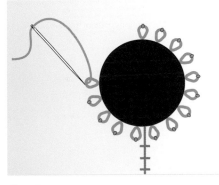

figure 3

14 Cut a 13 x 15-inch (33 x 38.1 cm) backing and a 12 1/2 x 4 1/2-inch (31.8 x 11.4 cm) hanging sleeve from the lavender fabric. Cut the remaining fabric on the true bias fabric grain into binding strips 1 1/2 inches (3.8 cm) wide. (The true bias grain runs at a 45° angle to the fabric selvage.)

15 Stack and baste the quilt layers. Thread the embroidery needle with two strands of light blue floss to quilt the sky in curving waves. Use green floss to quilt the hill in a meandering stipple design. Use the small needle and green sewing thread to sew bugle beads in a scattered arrangement on the hill.

16 Bind the quilt, using a 1/2-inch (1.3 cm) seam allowance. As you stitch the binding at each corner, shape the binding into a gentle curve.

17 Sew the hanging sleeve to the backing.

sparkling *heart*

This valentine of a mini-quilt sparkles with beads and snippets of shiny fabrics. A beautiful watercolor print cotton fabric establishes the vibrant color scheme, but you could use damask, hand-dyed silk dupioni, or a batik print if you prefer.

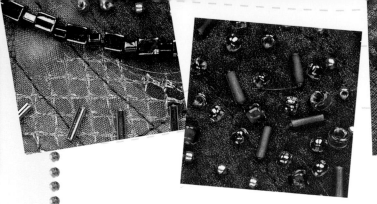

DESIGNER:
SHERRIE SPANGLER

FINISHED SIZE:
approximately 7 x 5 inches (17.8 x 12.7 cm)

Materials

Quilt top:
Cotton watercolor print fabric, 12 x 10 inches (30.5 x 25.4 cm)
Small snippets and ½ to 3-inch (3.8 to 7.6 cm) square
  pieces of assorted sheer and lustrous fabrics such as glitter
  organza, tulle, voile, metallic mesh, satin, and lamé

Beads:
About forty 4 mm (5/32 inch) cube-shaped metallic gold beads
About forty 8 mm (5/16 inch) hexagonal metallic purple beads
About 40 small gold bugle beads
About 12 small mixed pink and orange bugle beads
About 40 size 11/0 gold seed beads
About 40 size 8/0 and 6/0 seed beads in mixed colors

Batting:
Low-loft batting, 12 x 10 inches (30.5 x 25.4 cm)

Backing:
Muslin fabric, 12 x 10 inches (30.5 x 25.4 cm)

Thread, etc:
Light pink waxed nylon beading thread, size A
Pink 60 wt. polyester bobbin thread
Dark pink 40 wt. rayon embroidery thread
Pre-stretched canvas on a 7 x 5-inch (17.8 x 12.7 cm)
  wooden stretcher frame

Tools & Supplies

Sheet of paper with a 7 x 5-inch (17.8 x 12.7 cm)
  central cut-out
Tracing paper
Pencil
Beading needle
Staple gun

Templates

See page 121

Instructions

1 Stack and baste the quilt layers.

2 Pin the paper on the quilt top, centering the opening. The opening defines the area of the quilt to be embellished. Arrange the small snippets and squares of assorted fabrics in this area, cutting some of the fabrics into irregular shapes. Pin the fabrics in place, and then remove the paper.

3 Adjust the sewing machine for straight-stitch quilting. Thread the needle with rayon thread, and fill the bobbin with bobbin thread. Stitch gently curving lines on the quilt from side edge to side edge and from top edge to bottom edge. Stitch over the assorted fabrics as you go. Space the lines of quilting about ¼ to ½ inch (6 mm to 1.3 cm) apart.

4 Press the quilt, right side down.

5 Trace the heart template. Cut out the template. Pin it to the center of the embellished area.

DESIGNER Note: Experiment with the arrangement of the assorted small pieces of fabric on the quilt top to make a balanced composition. You can use one or more layers of sheer fabrics to intensify selected areas. For example, placing a red sheer fabric over pink, orange, or red background areas creates a rich red color.

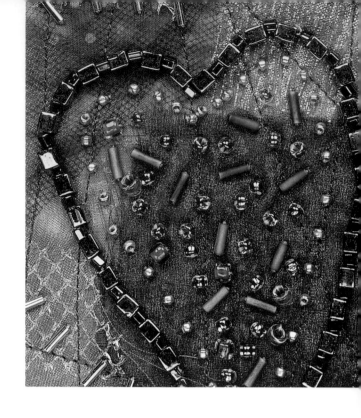

If you use bugle beads with smooth edges and sew them on the quilt with strong beading thread, you won't have to worry about thread breakage. If the bugle beads have sharp edges, you can add a seed bead at each end of a bugle bead to protect the thread.

6 Thread the beading needle with about 2 yards (1.8 m) of beading thread. Double the thread, and tie the ends in a knot. Bring the needle and thread through the quilt top from the backing at the cleft of the heart template. Use a backstitch to sew the first row of beads as an outline around the heart, alternating cube and hexagon beads. Remove the template. In the same way, sew two more rows of beads to outline the heart. Space the beads about 1/4 inch (6 mm) apart.

7 Use a seed stitch to sew the remaining beads in a scattered arrangement in the center of the heart.

8 Press the quilt, right side down.

9 Trim the quilt so it measures 9 x 8 inches (22.9 x 20.3 cm). Adjust the sewing machine for a narrow zigzag stitch. Stitch the raw edges of all the layers together around the outside of the quilt.

10 Use the staple gun to mount the quilt on the stretcher frame.

> " Beading this project was very meditative. I started with a simple line for the heart and echoed that shape with successive rows of different beads, but you could do as many rows as you like. "
> – SHERRIE SPANGLER, DESIGNER

Ancient
Cobblestones

The beads for this richly
textured quilt are assorted
washers and nuts from the
hardware store. They're
given an aged look by
sponging acrylic paints
lightly over the surface. Bits
of unusual materials such
as cheesecloth, handmade
paper, and pages from an old
book complete the design.

DESIGNER:
DEBORAH BOSCHERT

FINISHED SIZE:
approximately 39 x 9 inches (99.1 x 22.9 cm)

Materials

Quilt top:
About 10 assorted green and gold fabrics, each 6 to 10 inches (15.2 to 25.4 cm) square
2 yards (1.8 m) of fusible web, 20 inches (50.8 cm) wide
About five small pieces of novelty materials such as cheesecloth, organza, lace, handmade paper, and pages of text from an old book

Batting:
Low-loft cotton batting, 40 x 10 inches (101.6 x 25.4 cm)

Beads:
Washers: six 1-inch (2.5 cm) zinc, five ⅜-inch (9.5 mm) zinc, seventeen #8 brass, twenty-two #6 stainless steel, eight ⁵⁄₃₂-inch (4 mm) rubber, and four #10 nylon
Nuts: ten #8 square zinc

Backing:
Cotton fabric, 40 x 10 inches (101.6 x 25.4 cm)

Border:
Dark green wool felt, two pieces 40 x 3 inches (101.6 x 7.6 cm) and two pieces 10 x 3 inches (25.4 x 7.6 cm)

Thread, etc:
Gray and dark green sewing thread
Dark green embroidery floss
Two ¾-inch (1.9 cm) plastic rings

Tools & Supplies

Piece of paper
Green, black, and gold acrylic paint
Small natural sponge
Parchment paper
Glue stick
Black permanent marker
Digital camera (optional)
Embroidery needle with a large eye
Deckle-edge rotary cutter blade
Embroidery needle with a large eye
Hand-sewing needle
Fray retardant

Instructions

1 Follow the manufacturer's directions to apply fusible web to the wrong side of the quilt top fabrics and the backing fabric.

2 Cut the quilt top fabrics and novelty materials into free-form pieces about 2 inches (5 cm) square.

3 Arrange the squares of quilt top fabrics on parchment paper in 20 rows of four squares each. Place the squares right side up so the fusible side faces the parchment paper. Overlap the squares and the rows by about ⅛ inch (3 mm), and stagger the squares so the rows are uneven and the outer edges are irregular. Press the arrangement temporarily onto the parchment paper.

4 Add the squares of novelty materials as accents. Use them sparingly in just a few places. Glue the materials unsuitable for fusing such as paper and lace. Cover the quilt top with parchment paper, and press. Remove the layers of parchment paper.

5 Stack the quilt top on the batting. Use the permanent marker to trace around the edge of the quilt top. Trim the batting ¼ inch (6 mm) inside the traced line so the batting is smaller than the quilt top.

6 Stack the quilt top, right side down, and the batting; make sure the quilt extends by a margin of ¼ inch (6 mm) all around the batting. Cover with parchment paper, and press to fuse the quilt top to the batting.

> *Who knew the home improvement store could be such an incredible source for art supplies? I loved using the washers as embellishments on this quilt.* — DEBORAH BOSCHERT, DESIGNER

7 Adjust the sewing machine for free-motion quilting. Thread the needle and fill the bobbin with gray thread. Stitch a series of free-form stone shapes over the entire quilt top. Press the quilt.

8 Place the nuts and washers on the piece of paper. Use the sponge to dab a little of each color of paint on the nuts and washers. Use a light touch so some of the metal or rubber shows through the paint.

9 Arrange the nuts and washers on the quilt top. Place most of them on the lower half of the quilt in grids of two or three rows. Place some above to draw the eye up and over the entire quilt. Mix heavily painted washers with shinier ones. Draw a quick sketch or take a digital photo of the layout for reference. Remove the nuts and washers.

10 Thread the needle with two to four strands of floss. Sew the washers and nuts on the quilt top.

11 Stack the quilt right side up on the felt pieces. Arrange the felt pieces so a border of about 1/2 inch (1.3 cm) shows all around the quilt top. Cover the quilt with parchment paper, and press to fuse the quilt to the felt.

12 Adjust the sewing machine for straight stitching. Fill the bobbin with green thread. Topstitch through all layers about 1/4 inch (6 mm) from the edge of the quilt top.

13 Use the deckle-edge rotary cutter blade to trim the felt so it forms a border about 1/4 inch (6 mm) wide around the quilt top.

14 Stack the backing fabric, right side down, and the quilt, right side up. Use the marker to trace the felt border outline onto the backing. Trim the backing 1/2 inch (1.3 cm) smaller all around than the traced outline. Fuse the backing to the quilt.

15 Sew the rings to the upper corners of the backing.

DESIGNER *Note:* When arranging painted nuts and washers on the quilt, use the unpainted side where you prefer a shinier look. With nylon washers, you can see the paint through the washer even when it's attached with the painted side down, giving you creative options.

bumblebee
doll

This fascinating small quilt reinvents the doll as a handheld collage of stamped images, embroidery, and trinkets. The face appliqué, created on ink-jet printer cloth, could depict a favorite relative, child, or friend.

DESIGNER:

HEATHER NOBLITT

FINISHED SIZE:
approximately 9 inches (22.9 cm) square

Materials

Quilt top:
Rose cotton fabric, 9 inches (22.9 cm) square
Stiff nonwoven stabilizer, 9 inches (22.9 cm) square

Appliqué:
Sheet of ink-jet printer fabric
Digital image of girl's face
Paper-backed fusible web, 2 inches (5 cm) square

Backing:
Brown cotton fabric, 9 inches (22.9 cm) square

Beads:
Three pearl buttons, 1/8 inch (3 mm) in diameter
Four copper charms: two hands and two feet
Three 1-inch (2.5 cm) metal scrapbook letters: one *B*
    and two *Z*s

Thread, etc:
Brown and variegated rose embroidery floss
Assorted 6-inch (15.2 cm) pieces of novelty yarns, narrow
    ribbons, and narrow trims
Brown sewing thread

Tools & Supplies

Pencil
Stamp pad with brown pigment ink
Rubber stamps with small images of a bee, a key, and a
    clock face
Assorted colors of permanent fabric marking pens
Gold leaf pen
Computer with printer
Embroidery needle with a large eye
Fabric glue
Hand-sewing needle

Template

See page 121

Instructions

1 Trace the doll template onto the
    stabilizer. Stack the stabilizer, the quilt
top fabric, and the backing fabric. Pin them
together. Cut out all three layers 1/8 inch (3 mm)
larger than the traced outline. Trim the stabilizer
layer on the traced outline. Remove the pins, and
separate the fabric layers.

2 Follow the manufacturer's directions to print
    the face onto the ink-jet fabric, sizing the
image about 1 1/2 inches (3.8 cm) square.

3 Follow the web manufacturer's directions to
    fuse the face image to the quilt top 1/4 inch (6
mm) below the upper edge.

4 Stamp the quilt top with the bee, key, and
    clock images in a scattered, all-over design.
Color the images with the marking pens. Highlight
the bee wings with the gold pen.

5 Thread the embroidery needle with six strands of variegated floss. Outline the face with a stem stitch. Also embroider cross stitches in a scattered arrangement between the stamped images.

6 Stack and baste the quilt layers, using the stabilizer as the batting.

figure 2

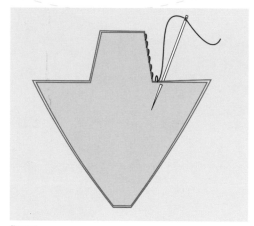

figure 1

7 Thread the embroidery needle with two strands of brown floss. Overcast the quilt layers together around the edge (see figure 1).

8 Sew the shoe and hand charms to the points of the quilt with a few hand stitches.

9 Glue the letters to the quilt top in a diagonal row. Glue a button to each letter.

10 Stack the assorted pieces of yarns, ribbons, and trims to create the doll's hair. Fold the stack in half, and sew several hand stitches near the fold to secure the stack (see figure 2). Sew the hair to the center top of the backing with several hand stitches.

UMBRELLA
abstracted

Change a bright orange umbrella appliqué into an artistic statement by slicing the image into small pieces and reassembling it as a small quilt. For the illusion of raindrops, sprinkle the angular rows of quilting with sequins and beads.

DESIGNER:
SARAH ANN SMITH

FINISHED SIZE:
approximately 9 x 11 inches (22.9 x 27.9 cm), mounted

Materials

Quilt top:

Blue hand-dyed or batik cotton fabric, 8 x 11 inches (20.3 x 27.9 cm)

Light, medium, and dark orange solid or print cotton fabrics, 3 x 7 inches (7.6 x 17.8 cm) of each

Green cotton fabric, 1/2 x 7 1/4 inches (1.3 x 18.4 cm)

1/2 yard (.5 m) of lightweight fusible web, 20 inches (50.8 cm) wide

Beads:

About 15 size 8/0 silver-lined orange seed beads

About 100 size 11/0 seed beads in assorted orange and yellow colors

About twenty 4 mm (5/32 inch) flat satin yellow sequins

About 30 assorted 4 to 6 mm (5/32 inch to 1/4 inch) round and square yellow iridescent sequins

About 12 small clear orange bugle beads

Batting:

Stiff polyester/rayon nonwoven interfacing, 5 1/2 x 7 1/2 inches (14 x 19 cm)

Backing:

Orange cotton fabric, 5 1/2 x 7 1/2 inches (14 x 19 cm)

Mounting:

Blue batik print cotton fabric, 16 x 18 inches (40.6 x 45.7 cm)

Low-loft batting, 16 x 18 inches (40.6 x 45.7 cm)

Two 9 x 11-inch (22.9 x 27.9 cm) wood stretcher frames

Thread, etc:

Orange 40 wt. polyester machine embroidery thread

Orange 60 wt. polyester bobbin thread

1 yard (.9 m) of blue cotton yarn

Blue sewing thread

Tools & Supplies

Parchment paper
Graphite transfer paper
Pencil
Small hand-sewing needle for beading
Staple gun

Templates

See page 122

Instructions

1 Follow the manufacturer's instructions to apply fusible web to the blue, orange, and green fabrics for the quilt top. Also apply web to the backing fabric.

2 Use graphite paper and a pencil to transfer the umbrella appliqué templates to the orange fabrics. Cut out the appliqué pieces.

3 Cut out a 7 x 3/8-inch (17.8 cm x 9.5 mm) umbrella pole appliqué from green fabric.

4 Cut out a 5 x 7-inch (12.7 x 17.8 cm) appliqué base and a 5 1/2 x 7 1/2-inch (14 x 19 cm) quilt top from blue fabric.

5 Stack the quilt top right side up on the interfacing, and fuse.

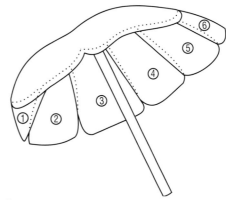

figure 1

6 Lay the appliqué base right side up on a piece of parchment paper. Arrange the umbrella and pole appliqués on the base, overlapping the appliqués as indicated on the templates (see figure 1). Note that the larger umbrella top overlay appliqué is fused over the smaller umbrella top appliqué to prevent shadow-through of the other fabrics. Fuse the appliqués to the base fabric, and remove the base fabric from the parchment paper.

figure 2

7 Cut the appliqué and base fabric apart into chunks and slices (see figure 2). Arrange these pieces into a pleasing composition on the quilt top. Overlap the appliqué pieces as you make an arrangement that balances the orange and blue colors. Cut some of the blue pieces into small bits and wedges from $1/2$ to $1 1/2$ inches (1.3 to 3.8 cm), and then arrange them on top of some of the larger orange pieces. Note that you do not have to use every piece of fabric in the composition, and you will probably have extra blue pieces left over. Fuse the arrangement to the quilt top.

8 Adjust the sewing machine for straight-stitch quilting. Thread the needle with embroidery thread, and fill the bobbin with bobbin thread. Stitch straight lines in an angular, free-form design over the quilt top. If available on your sewing machine, select a decorative stitch pattern such as satin-stitched triangles. Stitch single and double groups of triangles in any open spaces in the quilting design.

9 Thread the hand-sewing needle with bobbin thread, doubled. Sew a sequin with a seed bead stacked on top in clusters of three and five scattered across the quilt; at times stack two kinds of sequins before adding the seed bead. Sew the following elements where desired: individual sequin/seed bead combinations, bugle beads with seed beads at each end, and individual or short rows of seed beads. Place all beads $3/4$ inch (1.9 cm) from the raw edges of the quilt.

10 Fuse the backing fabric to the quilt. Trim the quilt to 5 x 7 inches (12.7 x 17.8 cm).

11 Couch yarn around the edge of the quilt with blue sewing thread, stitching by hand or using a machine zigzag stitch.

12 Stack the stretcher frames. Join the frames together by stapling each side with a few vertical staples that bridge both frames. Stack the batting and the mounting fabric. Staple them to the frame.

13 Sew the quilt to the center of the fabric-covered frame.

"My art tends to be representational, but I wanted to learn more about making non-representational or abstract art. Created for a group project, this piece began with a photo of an orange umbrella at the beach. — **SARAH ANN SMITH, DESIGNER**

love letters

This quilt is a fresh interpretation of a traditional nine-patch pattern. The addition of the borders creates an asymmetric composition that also forms a big "L" for love. The quilting and beading motifs represent handwritten hugs and kisses.

DESIGNER:
DEBORAH BOSCHERT

FINISHED SIZE:
approximately 25 x 19 inches (63.5 x 48.3 cm)

Materials

Quilt top:
12 assorted cotton print fabrics, each 4 ½ x 5 ½ inches
   (11.4 x 14 cm)
Blue batik cotton fabric, 20 ½ x 5 ½ inches (52 x 14 cm)
   and 20 ½ x 3 ¼ inches (52 x 8.3 cm)
15 assorted cotton print fabrics, each 2 x 1 ½ to 3 inches
   (5 x 3.8 to 7.6 cm)

Batting:
Low-loft batting, 27 x 21 inches (68.6 x 53.3 cm)

Backing:
Cotton fabric, 28 x 22 inches (71.1 x 55.9 cm)

Beads:
About 300 seed beads of each color. green, fuchsia, and teal

Binding:
Pink batik cotton fabric, three 45 x 1-inch (114.3 x 2.5 cm)
   strips

Hanging sleeve:
Cotton fabric, 18 ½ x 4 ½ inches (47 x 11.4 cm)

Thread, etc:
Purple sewing thread
Green, fuchsia, and teal nylon beading thread, size D

Tools & Supplies

Small hand-sewing needle for beading

¼-inch (6 mm) seam allowance

Instructions

1 Arrange the 12 assorted fabrics in four rows
of three pieces each with the longer sides
touching. Sew the pieces in each row together. Press
the seam allowances to one side, alternating the
direction with each row. Sew the rows together for the
quilt top. Press the seams toward the bottom row.

2 Sew the 5 ½-inch-wide (14 cm) blue piece on
the left-hand side of the quilt top with right
sides together. Press the seam toward the blue fabric.

3 Sew the other blue piece on the bottom of the
quilt top with right sides together. Press the
seam toward the blue fabric.

4 Sew the 15 assorted print fabrics together
to make a border at least 20 ½ inches long
(52 cm). Press the seams to one side. Sew the
border to the bottom of the quilt top with right sides
together. Press the seam away from the border.

5 Stack and baste the quilt layers.

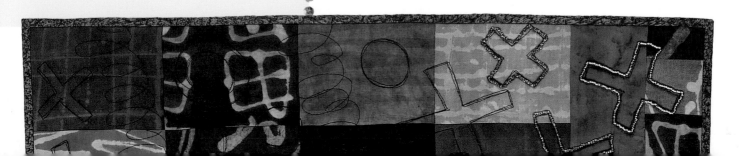

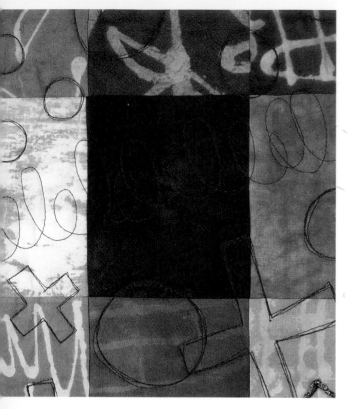

6 Adjust the sewing machine for free-motion quilting. Thread the needle and fill the bobbin with purple thread. Stitch looping lines that suggest handwriting. Add several circles and *X* shapes, stitching over each two or three times roughly. If desired, echo some of the print motifs in the pieced section of the quilt top with the stitching. Press the quilt.

7 Thread the hand-sewing needle with thread to match each bead color. Use a backstitch to outline a few of the quilting motifs with a row of beads.

8 Bind the quilt, using a 1/4-inch (6 mm) seam allowance and mitered corners.

9 Attach the hanging sleeve.

"The free-motion quilting in this piece has a 'sketchy' quality about it. Rather than outline a motif just once with precise stitches, I traced over it several times, making it look more spontaneous and intentionally untidy."

– DEBORAH BOSCHERT, DESIGNER

VINTAGE *pillow*

This beaded pillow offers a creative opportunity to "up cycle" vintage odds and ends. The patchwork could consist of nostalgic fabrics harvested from childhood clothing, a treasured dresser scarf, or a memory-laden kitchen tablecloth.

DESIGNER:
JOAN K. MORRIS

FINISHED SIZE:
approximately 13 inches (33 cm) square

Materials

Pillow top:
Nine assorted fabric pieces
Several pieces of vintage lace
1/2 yard (.5 m) of lace edging, 1/2 inch (1.3 cm) wide

Backing:
Muslin fabric, 15 inches (38.1 cm) square

Batting:
Low-loft cotton batting, 15 inches (38.1 cm) square

Pillow back:
Off-white upholstery fabric, 15 inches (38.1 cm) square

Beads*:
48 size 6/0 (also called E beads) seed beads, each: clear,
    blue, green, turquoise, and orange
100 size 6/0 seed beads, each: green, yellow, red, purple,
    turquoise, and pearl
36 small green bugle beads
1 pink and two green 3/4-inch (1.9 cm) buttons
Three 1/2-inch (1.3 cm) green glass flower beads

* Bead quantities are approximate

Thread, etc:
Off-white, blue, green, orange, purple, and yellow sewing thread
Black, orange, and pink embroidery floss
Polyester fiberfill

Tools & Supplies

Scrap paper 15 inches (38.1 cm) square
Embroidery needle with a large eye
Beading needle

1/4-inch (6 mm) seam allowance unless noted otherwise

Instructions

1   Cut the assorted fabric scraps into squares and
    rectangles. Arrange them in three rows in a
pleasing design, using the scrap paper as a template
for the size of the pillow top. To allow for 1/4-inch
(6 mm) seams, overlap the squares and rectangles
by 1/2 inch (1.3 cm) as you arrange them.

2   Adjust the sewing machine for a straight
    stitch. Thread the needle and fill the bobbin
with off-white thread. Sew the pieces in each row
with right sides together. Press the seams open. Sew
the rows together to make the pillow top. Press the
seams open.

3   Place the lace edging over some of the pillow
    top seams. Sew both edges of the lace to the
pillow top.

4   Arrange the vintage lace pieces on the pillow
    top. Adjust the sewing machine for a zigzag
stitch of medium length and narrow width. Sew the
edges of the lace to the pillow top.

5   Stack and baste the quilt layers, using the
    pillow top as the quilt top.

6   Adjust the sewing machine for straight-stitch
    quilting. Follow the fabric designs in each
pillow top fabric as you quilt the layers together; for
example, stitch a grid of squares on plaid fabric, and
use shaped rows of quilting to echo floral motifs.

7   Thread an embroidery needle with six strands
    of floss. Adding a seed bead with every
stitch or every other stitch, embroider decorative
buttonhole, cross, and running stitches along the
patchwork seams.

8 Mark the placement for the buttons and flower beads. To avoid snagging the beading thread, wait to sew the buttons and flower beads in place until after you have beaded the pillow top.

9 Use the beading needle and a thread color to match the beads to sew the remaining beads on the pillow top. Start in the center, and sew the beads in a decorative design to accent each pillow top fabric; for example, cover floral motifs with color-matched beads, and sew a single contrasting bead in the center of each dot on polka dot fabric. After sewing several beads in place with a single length of thread, sew a knot on the wrong side of the pillow top to secure the beads before you continue sewing.

10 Sew the buttons and flower beads on the pillow top.

11 Stack the pillow top and the pillow back with right sides together. Trim them so they are 14 inches (35.6 cm) square. Sew the edges in a 1/2-inch (1.3 cm) seam, leaving an opening for turning along one edge.

12 Trim diagonally across the corners. Turn the pillow right side out.

13 Insert fiberfill through the opening to fill the pillow. Close the opening with small hand stitches.

jewels of our *past*

This pieced quilt features a series of round appliqués in three graduated sizes. They're padded with stabilizer, covered with fabric, and encrusted with beads to look like ancient treasure unearthed in the desert.

Materials

Quilt top:
Hand-dyed and batik cotton fabrics, about 14 assorted pieces
   (see figure 1 for actual sizes of the pieces)
Muslin fabric, 31 x 16 inches (78.7 x 40.6 cm)

Batting:
Low-loft batting, 31 x 16 inches (78.7 x 40.6 cm)

Beaded appliqués:
1/8 yard (.1 m) of stiff polyester/rayon stabilizer, 22 inches
   (55.9 cm) wide
1/8 yard (.1 m) of turquoise fabric, any width
9 assorted beads, about 1/2 inch (1.3 cm) in diameter
About 2,000 assorted beads: blue, green, and purple seed
   beads; small bugle beads; and small crystal beads

Backing and hanging sleeve:
1/2 yard (.5 m) of cotton fabric, 44 inches (111.8 cm) wide

Thread, etc:
Turquoise sewing thread
Rust and variegated red/brown polyester quilting thread
Blue, green, and purple nylon beading thread, size D

Tools & Supplies

Freezer paper
Pencil
Small hand-sewing needle for beading
#2 beading needle
Fabric glue

Templates

See page 122

1/4-inch (6 mm) seam allowance

Instructions

1 Cut the pieces for the quilt top from the
assorted fabrics (see figure 1). Sew the pieces
together in the sequence shown.

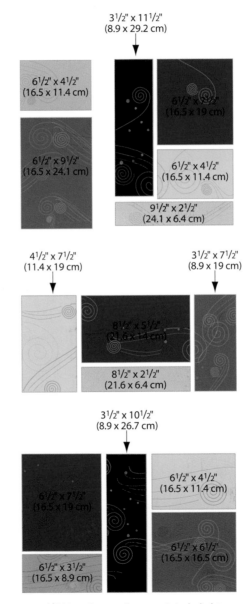

3 1/2" x 11 1/2"
(8.9 x 29.2 cm)

6 1/2" x 4 1/2"
(16.5 x 11.4 cm)

6 1/2" x 7 1/2"
(16.5 x 19 cm)

6 1/2" x 9 1/2"
(16.5 x 24.1 cm)

6 1/2" x 4 1/2"
(16.5 x 11.4 cm)

9 1/2" x 2 1/2"
(24.1 x 6.4 cm)

4 1/2" x 7 1/2"
(11.4 x 19 cm)

3 1/2" x 7 1/2"
(8.9 x 19 cm)

8 1/2" x 5 1/2"
(21.6 x 14 cm)

8 1/2" x 2 1/2"
(21.6 x 6.4 cm)

3 1/2" x 10 1/2"
(8.9 x 26.7 cm)

6 1/2" x 7 1/2"
(16.5 x 19 cm)

6 1/2" x 4 1/2"
(16.5 x 11.4 cm)

6 1/2" x 6 1/2"
(16.5 x 16.5 cm)

6 1/2" x 3 1/2"
(16.5 x 8.9 cm)

1/4" (6 mm) seam allowance is included

figure 1

2 Stack the muslin, the batting, and the quilt top, right side up. Baste the layers together with safety pins.

3 Adjust the sewing machine for free-motion quilting. Thread the needle and fill the bobbin with either color of quilting thread. Stitch an all-over design of swirling rows, using rust thread for some of the rows and variegated red/brown for some of the rows.

4 Trim the quilt top to 29 1/2 x 14 1/2 inches (73.7 x 36.8 cm), squaring off the corners.

5 Trace the templates onto freezer paper with a pencil. Cut each size of template three times from the stabilizer for the appliqué bases. Cut each size of template three times from the turquoise fabric for the appliqué covers.

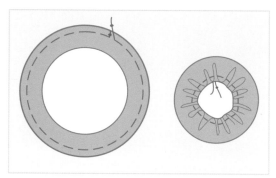

6 Sew running stitches around each appliqué cover. Place the corresponding appliqué base in the center on the wrong side, and pull the thread to gather the cover around the base (see figure 2). Secure the gathers with a few small stitches, and trim the thread tails.

figure 2

7 Thread the sewing needle with beading thread. To encrust each appliqué with beads, sew a large bead at or near the center of the fabric-covered base, and then sew assorted beads to surround the large bead. Arrange the beads in a different design on each appliqué. Fill in any spaces with single seed beads. Use the beading needle to sew the smallest beads.

DESIGNER Note: Gather a great variety of small beads to surround the large focal bead on each appliqué. Find several kinds of beads such as seed beads–in size 12/0 and smaller–and seed beads with triangle and hexagon shapes. Add to the mix a few different lengths of bugle beads, an assortment of rondelles, and some sparkling crystals.

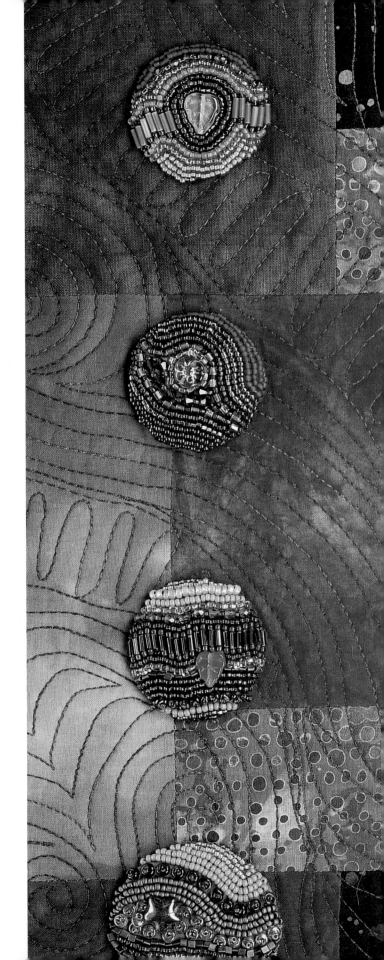

> "I spend a fair amount of time choosing my color scheme. Then I try hard not to second-guess myself. If I try to re-select my colors partway through the project, I generally end up with a muddier, less satisfying range of color."
> – LARKIN JEAN VAN HORN , DESIGNER

8 Arrange the appliqués on the quilt top 1 3/4 inches (4.4 cm) apart in a vertical row 4 1/4 inches (10.8 cm) from the left side edge of the quilt top. Put the three smallest appliqués at the top of the row, the three midsized appliqués in the center, and the three largest appliqués at the bottom. Glue the center back of each appliqué to the quilt. Let the glue dry. Sew the outer edge of each appliqué to the quilt top with small hand stitches.

9 Cut two sections from the backing fabric, a backing that measures 29 1/2 x 14 1/2 inches (74.9 x 36.8 cm) and a hanging sleeve that is 4 1/2 x 13 1/2 inches (11.4 x 34.3 cm).

10 Stack the backing and the quilt top with right sides together. Stitch around the edge, leaving an opening along the bottom. Trim the four corners diagonally to reduce bulk in the seam allowances. Turn the quilt right side out through the opening. Close the opening with hand stitches.

11 Sew the hanging sleeve to the backing.

TEA TIME
apron

The apron, equal parts cloth and comfort, goes upscale when you decorate it with beaded appliqués inspired by high tea. The roomy pocket has three compartments for storing utensils, a hankie, or perhaps some wrapped peppermints.

DESIGNER:
JOAN K. MORRIS

FINISHED SIZE:
approximately 27 x 24 inches (68.6 x 61 cm)

Materials

Apron:
⅞ yard (.8 m) each of green and tan cotton fabrics, 44 inches (111.8 cm) wide

Appliqués:
Five assorted blue and white, pink, and orange cotton print fabric strips 24 x 1 to 2 inches (61 x 2.5 to 5 cm)
White cotton fabric, 5 inches (12.7 cm) square
Vintage doily fragment, 7 x 6 inches (17.8 x 15.2 cm)
Paper-backed fusible web: 24 x 7 inches (61 x 17.8 cm),
    7 x 6 inches (17.8 x 15.2 cm), and 5 inches (12.7 cm) square

Beads:
One 1-inch (2.5 cm) blue-and-white bead
One ½-inch (1.3 cm) blue glass bead
2 orange glass flower beads
Size 10/0 or 11/0 seed beads*: 30 blue glass, 180 orange, 175 pearl, 25 silver, and 100 brown metallic
*80 size 6/0 (also called E-beads) brown seed beads
*Sixty ¼-inch (6 mm) clear bugle beads

Bead quantities are approximate

Backing:
⅞ yard (.8 m) of muslin fabric, 44 inches (111.8 cm) wide

Batting:
Low-loft batting, 31 x 27 inches (78.7 x 68.6 cm)

Thread, etc:
Green, tan, white, blue, orange, and brown sewing thread
Clear monofilament nylon thread

Tools & Supplies

Large piece of scrap paper
Pencil
Chalk fabric marker
Small hand-sewing needle for beading

Templates

See page 123

Instructions

1 Draw the apron pattern on scrap paper (see figure 1).

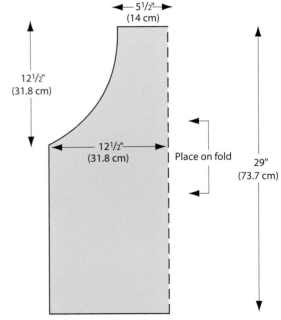

← 5½" →
(14 cm)

12½"
(31.8 cm)

12½"
(31.8 cm)

Place on fold

29"
(73.7 cm)

½" (1.3 cm) seam allowance included

figure 1

2 Cut the apron pattern once each from green fabric for the apron front, tan fabric for the apron lining, muslin for the backing, and batting. From tan fabric, also cut two pockets 9 x 21 inches (22.9 x 53.3 cm), a neck tie 29 x 1½ inches (73.7 x 3.8 cm), and two waist ties each 30 x 2½ inches (76.2 x 6.4 cm).

3 Trace the contrast appliqué templates onto the paper backing of the 5-inch (12.7 cm) square of fusible web. Follow the manufacturer's directions to apply the fusible web to the white fabric. Cut out the appliqués.

4 Sew the assorted fabric strips together using a ¼-inch (6 mm) seam allowance. After sewing the strips together, the pieced panel should measure at least 24 x 6 inches (61 x 15.2 cm). Press the seams open.

5 Trace the remaining appliqué templates onto the paper backing of the 24 x 7-inch (61 x 17.8 cm) piece of fusible web. Follow the manufacturer's directions to apply fusible web to the wrong side of the pieced panel. Cut out the appliqués.

6 Follow the manufacturer's directions to apply the remaining fusible web to the wrong side of the doily fragment. Fuse the doily on an angle to the apron bib.

7 Adjust the sewing machine for straight stitching. Thread the needle with nylon thread. Fill the bobbin with green thread. Stitch the doily around the edge and around any central design.

8 Fuse the teapot and teapot lid appliqués to the bib so they overlap the doily. Adjust the sewing machine for zigzag stitching, selecting a short stitch length and narrow width. Stitch over the raw edges of the appliqués.

9 Mark two stitching lines on one pocket section (see figure 2). Fuse the cup, saucer, and cup contrast appliqués to the center area. Fuse the creamer and creamer contrast appliqués on the left-hand area and the sugar bowl, lid, and sugar bowl contrast on the right-hand area. Zigzag stitch over the raw edges of the appliqués as in step 8, but fill the bobbin with tan thread.

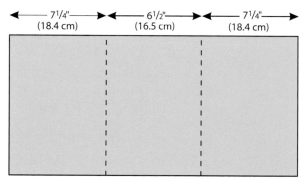

| ←——7¼"——→ | ←——6½"——→ | ←——7¼"——→ |
| (18.4 cm) | (16.5 cm) | (18.4 cm) |

figure 2

10 Thread the hand-sewing needle with sewing thread to match each color of seed bead. Use a backstitch to sew the size 6/0 beads in rows on the coffee cup contrast. Use a seed stitch to sew pearl beads on the creamer contrast and silver beads on the sugar bowl contrast. On each corner of the doily, stack an orange seed bead on an orange flower bead, and sew them in place. Sew the remaining seed beads on the appliqués, using a backstitch or seed stitch and following the print motifs in the fabrics for the beading designs.

11 Sew the blue glass bead to the center top of the sugar bowl lid.

12 Sew bugle beads individually in three curling rows above the coffee cup to represent steam.

13 Stack and baste the quilt layers, using the green apron front as the quilt top and muslin as the backing.

14 Adjust the sewing machine for straight-stitch quilting. Install a quilting bar attachment. Stitch a diagonal grid of diamonds on the entire apron, spacing the rows of stitches 1 1/2 inches (3.8 cm) apart. Do not stitch over the doily and teapot appliqués.

15 Thread the hand-sewing needle with white thread. Sew bugle beads individually in two curling rows coming from the teapot spout and two rows coming from the open teapot lid. Sew the blue-and-white bead to the center top of the teapot lid.

16 Place the pocket sections with right sides together. Sew around the edges, leaving an opening on the bottom edge. Trim the corners diagonally to reduce bulk. Turn the pocket right side out through the opening. Press the pocket. Sew the opening closed with small hand stitches.

17 Pin the pocket, appliqué side up, 5 1/2 inches (14 cm) above the bottom center of the apron. Adjust the sewing machine for straight stitching. Thread the needle and fill the bobbin with tan thread. Topstitch next to the edge of the pocket on the sides and the bottom. Topstitch on the marked lines between the appliqués.

18 Fold each neck and waist tie in half with wrong sides together along its length. Press the fold. Open each tie out flat. Fold each long raw edge to the pressed fold, and press. Fold each tie in half along its length, and press. Topstitch close to the open edge of each tie.

19 Pin the ends of the neck tie 1/2 inch (1.3 cm) from each top corner of the bib. Pin one end of a waist tie 1/2 inch (1.3 cm) below each side corner. Machine-baste the ties in place.

20 Stack the tan lining and the apron with right sides together. Pin the ties away from the edges so only the ends of the ties extend into the seam allowance. Stitch the seam around the edge of the apron, leaving an opening along the bottom edge. Clip the curved seam allowances. Trim diagonally across the corners to reduce bulk. Turn the apron right side out through the opening. Close the opening with small hand stitches. Press the edge of the apron.

21 Thread the sewing machine needle with nylon thread. Topstitch the apron 1/2 inch (1.3 cm) from the edge.

22 Fold over the raw end of each waist tie 1/2 inch (1.3 cm) two times. Sew the hem with small hand stitches.

forest fern *quilt*

This quilt seems like a living forest with its vines, ferns, and woodland blossoms sparkling with big, bold beads. The largest beads are originals you create by cutting out modeling clay with the twist-off cap from a bottle of water.

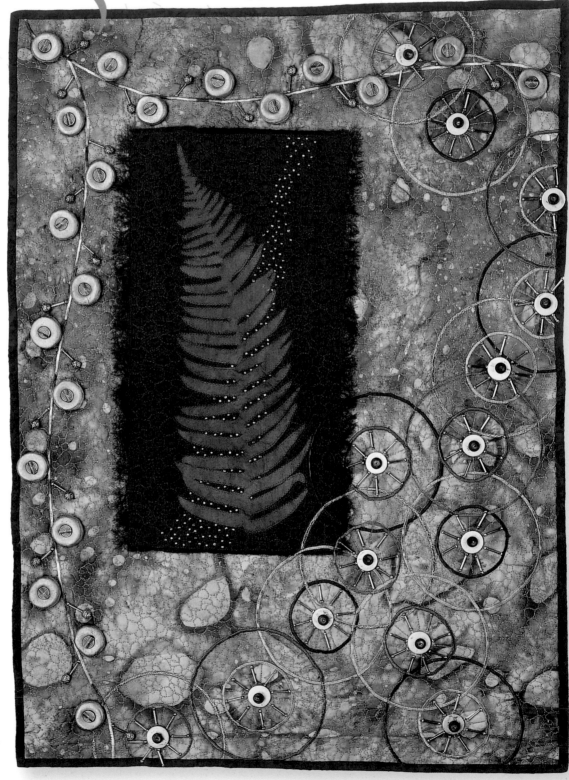

Materials

Quilt top:
Green cotton fabric, 28 x 21 inches (71.1 x 53.3 cm)

Appliqué:
Blue silk fabric, 15 ½ x 8 ½ inches (39.4 x 21.6 cm)
Brown cotton fabric, 15 x 6 inches (38.1 x 15.2 cm)
Paper-backed fusible web, 15 x 6 inches (38.1 x 15.2 cm)

Beads:
Fourteen ¾-inch (1.9 cm) center-drilled beige disk beads
Fourteen ⅜-inch (9.5 mm) center-drilled blue disk beads
14 size 10/0 or 11/0 green seed beads
About one hundred twenty-seven ½-inch (1.3 cm) gold
    bugle beads
Twenty ½-inch (1.3 cm) side-drilled copper disk beads
Size 11/0 seed beads: 14 green, about 250 silver, and about
    350 metallic gold
Nineteen ¼-inch (6 mm) round metallic gold beads

Backing and hanging sleeve:
⅞ yard (.8 m) of green print cotton fabric, 44 inches
    (111.8 cm) wide

Batting:
Low-loft batting, 30 x 23 inches (76.2 x 58.4 cm)

Binding:
¼ yard (.2 m) of blue cotton fabric, 44 inches (111.8 cm) wide

Thread, etc:
Clear monofilament nylon thread
Blue and beige sewing thread
Green and blue cotton machine quilting thread
40 wt. rayon machine embroidery thread in five shades of tan,
    gold, and brown
40 wt. variegated gold rayon machine embroidery thread
Tear-away stabilizer, two pieces 28 x 21 inches
    (71.1 x 53.3 cm)
2 ounces of air-dry modeling clay

Tools & Supplies

Large sheet of tracing paper
Pencil
Masking tape
Window
Bronze or copper acrylic paint
Small paintbrush
Evaporating ink fabric marker
Embroidery needle with a large eye
Small hand-sewing needle for beading
Bottle cap about 1 inch (2.5 cm) in diameter
Stiletto or large needle
Wax paper

Templates

See page 124

¼-inch (6 mm) seam allowance

DESIGNER:
JULIA DONALDSON

FINISHED SIZE:
approximately 27 x 20 inches (68.6 x 50.8 cm)

Instructions

1 Trace the fern template onto the paper side of the fusible web. Follow the manufacturer's directions to apply the web to the wrong side of the brown fabric. Cut out the fern appliqué. Peel off the paper backing, and fuse the appliqué to the center of the blue silk fabric.

2 Adjust the sewing machine for zigzag stitching, selecting a short length and a narrow width. Thread the needle with monofilament nylon thread. Fill the bobbin with blue sewing thread. Stitch around the edges of the fern appliqué.

3 Pin the appliquéd blue fabric to the quilt top 4 ¾ (12.1 cm) inches below the upper edge and 4 ¾ (12.1 cm) inches from the left-hand side of the quilt top. Adjust the sewing machine for straight stitching. Thread the needle with blue sewing thread. Topstitch the blue fabric ½ inch (1.3 cm) in from the raw edge all around. Pull the loose threads from the raw edges of the blue fabric to create a soft fringe.

4 Trace the embroidery template onto tracing paper. Pin the traced template to the wrong side of the quilt top, and then tape them to a window. Use the fabric marker to transfer the embroidery placement lines from the traced template to the quilt top. Remove the traced template.

5 Pin the two layers of stabilizer to the wrong side of the quilt top. Adjust the sewing machine for zigzag stitching, using the settings for satin stitching as recommended in your sewing machine manual. Select a stitch length short enough so the stitches form very closely together and look like a solid outline without the fabric showing through the stitches; select a stitch width that measures a scant $1/8$ inch (3 mm). To stitch the vine on the left-hand side and along the upper portion of the quilt top, thread the needle with variegated thread, and fill the bobbin with beige thread. To stitch the circles, thread the needle, in turn, with each of the five shades of tan, gold, and brown embroidery thread. Stitch around the circles in a clockwise direction. To pivot the quilt top as you stitch, stop sewing with the needle down in the fabric as it makes a right-hand swing (see figure 1), raise the presser foot, and turn the quilt top. If available on your model, use the sewing machine setting to lock the stitches at the start and finish of each circle, or leave long thread tails to thread through the embroidery needle so you can bring them to the wrong side of the quilt top and tie them in a knot.

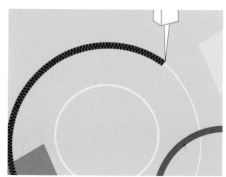

figure 1

6 Remove the stabilizer. Press the quilt top, right side down.

7 Cut a backing that measures 31 x 25 inches (78.7 x 63.5 cm) from green print fabric. From the remaining fabric, cut a hanging sleeve that is 19 x 4 $1/2$ inches (48.3 x 11.4 cm), and reserve.

8 Stack and baste the quilt layers.

9 Adjust the sewing machine for free-motion quilting. Thread the needle with blue cotton quilting thread, and fill the bobbin with green quilting thread. Stitch the blue background around the fern appliqué in a meandering, circular design with circles about $1/4$ to $1/2$ inch (6 to 13 mm) in diameter. In the same way, thread the needle with green cotton quilting thread to stitch the remainder of the quilt; stitch a design of eight spokes within each of the smaller circles.

10 Lay a sheet of wax paper on the work surface. Place the modeling clay on the wax paper. Smooth out the clay to make a slab $1/4$-inch (6 mm) thick. Use the bottle cap to cut out 20 beads. Use the stiletto or large needle to release the clay from the bottle cap if necessary.

11 Smooth out the edge of each clay bead with your finger. Press a copper disk bead in the center of each clay bead to leave an imprint deep enough to allow the copper bead to sit flush with the surface of the clay bead. Remove the copper beads. Use the stiletto or large needle to pierce a hole in the center of each clay bead. Follow the manufacturer's directions to let the clay beads dry.

12 Place a dab of bronze or copper paint on the wax paper next to the clay beads. Paint all surfaces of each bead with a small paintbrush. Let the beads dry on the wax paper.

13 Trim the quilt to 27 x 20 inches (68.6 x 50.8 cm).

14 Cut binding strips 1 inch (2.5 cm) wide from blue cotton fabric. Bind the quilt, using a 1/4-inch (6 mm) seam allowance and mitered corners.

15 Thread the small needle for beading with beige thread, doubled. In the center of each of the smaller circles, stack a green seed bead, a blue disk bead, and a beige disk bead; sew them with a single stitch, then repeat the stitch to sew the stack securely to the quilt (see figure 2). Using the same thread, sew eight bugle beads like spokes in each small circle, using a gold seed bead at each end of each bugle bead; then repeat the stitch to secure the beads (see figure 3). As you stitch the beads in place, arrange some of them to overlap the binding.

figure 2

16 Arrange the clay beads evenly along the vine. Use the fabric marker to mark the bead positions. To sew each clay bead, bring the needle up through the clay bead, then bring it through a copper disk bead and back through the clay bead to the quilt backing. Repeat this stitch two more times to secure the beads.

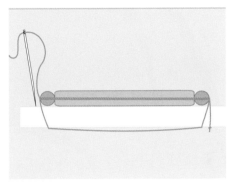

figure 3

17 Sew a gold seed bead, a bugle bead, and a round gold bead to the vine between each clay bead. Sew back through each set of beads a second time to secure them (see figure 4).

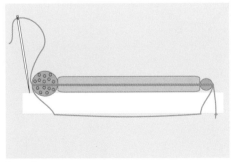

figure 4

18 Use a seed stitch to sew the gold and silver seed beads around the fern appliqué. Arrange the beads in a scattered design that begins near the lower left-hand corner of the blue silk fabric and stretches diagonally up to the opposite corner.

19 Attach the hanging sleeve.

TAG-ALONG *handbag*

Explore nine ways to use beads on a quilt as you create this delightful casual handbag. It's a virtual sampler of beading techniques sewn to a background made from a pieced log cabin quilt block.

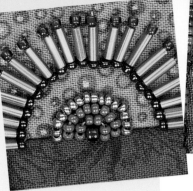
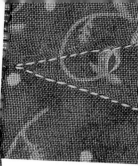

DESIGNER:
VERONICA HOFMAN ORTEGA

FINISHED SIZE:
approximately 9 x 8 inches (22.9 x 20.3 cm), plus strap

Materials

Handbag front:

(A) Black/white/gray flower motif from cotton fabric, 2 ½-inch (6.4 cm) square

(B) Medium green print cotton fabric and medium brown print cotton fabric, one 2 ½ x 1 ½-inch strip of each (6.4 x 3.8 cm)

(C) Dark brown cotton fabric and burnt orange cotton fabric, one 1 ½ x 4 ½-inch strip of each (3.8 x 11.4 cm)

(D) Two green print fabric strips, each 4 ½ x 2 ¾ inches (11.4 x 7 cm)

(E) Rose print and brown print cotton fabrics, one 3 ½ x 9-inch (8.9 x 22.9 cm) strip of each

Handbag back:

(A) Black/white/gray fashion-figure cotton fabric print, 6 ½ x 3 ½ inches (16.5 x 8.9 cm)

Medium brown print cotton fabric strips:
  (B) 6 ½ x 1 ½ inches (16.5 x 3.8 cm),
  (G) 5 ½ x 3 ¾ inches (14 x 9.5 cm), and
  (H) 2 ¼ x 9 inches (5.7 x 22.9 cm)

(C) Dark brown cotton fabric strip, 6 ½ x 1 ¾ inches (16.5 x 4.5 cm)

(D, F) Two green and burnt orange print fabric strips, each 2 ¼ x 3 ¾ inches (5.7 x 9.5 cm)

(E) Rose print cotton fabric strip, 1 ½ x 3 ¾ inches (3.8 x 9.5 cm)

Flap and button loop:

Purple print cotton fabric, two pieces 8 x 4 inches (20.3 x 10.2 cm)

Olive green print fabric, 1 ¼ x 5-inch (3.2 x 12.7 cm) strip cut on the true bias fabric grain

Shoulder strap:

Brown print cotton fabric, 38 x 3-inch (96.5 x 7.6 cm) strip

Beads*:

Seed beads, size 11/0: about 12 topaz matte, 41 metallic turquoise, 15 yellow/lime, 30 pewter opaque, 230 olive green opaque, 100 blackberry brandy, and 255 dark purple opaque luster

5 size 8/0 purple seed beads

16 size 6/0 blue matte metallic seed beads

80 size 10/0 orange opaque seed beads

25 size 6/0 mustard marble swirl seed beads

Forty ¼-inch (6 mm) topaz matte bugle beads

6 novelty circular beads with a flower motif

5 teardrop-shaped red beads

Sew-through decorative button, about 1 inch (2.5 cm) in diameter

½-inch (1.3 cm) purple glass bead

Bead quantities are approximate

Backing:

Muslin fabric, two pieces 10 x 9 inches (25.4 x 22.9 cm)

Batting:

Low-loft batting, two pieces 10 x 9 inches (25.4 x 22.9 cm) for the purse front and back, and one piece 8 x 4 inches (20.3 x 10.2 cm) for the flap

Lining:

Yellow print cotton fabric, two pieces 9 ¾ x 8 ¾ inches (24.8 x 22.2 cm)

Thread, etc:

Brown sewing thread
Brown and variegated orange cotton machine quilting thread
Brown nylon beading thread, size D

Tools & Supplies

Hand-sewing needle for beading
Beading needle

¼-inch (6 mm) seam allowance unless noted otherwise

DESIGNER *Note:* For a more formal version of the handbag, substitute deluxe fabrics such as brocade or silk dupioni for the cotton fabrics. Instead of a self-fabric strap, you could use embroidered ribbon or decorative cord. Whether you create a casual or a formal handbag, you have the option of adding beads to the back.

Front

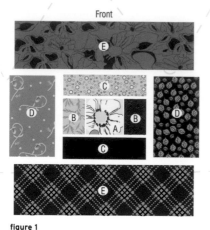

Back

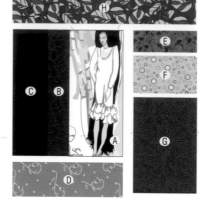

figure 1

Instructions

1 Begin with the center section to piece the log cabin block for the front and back of the handbag, following the alphabetical sequence indicated in figure 1.

2 Trim the handbag front and back so each measures 10 x 9 inches (25.4 x 22.9 cm).

3 Stack the quilt layers for the handbag, making a stack for the front and a stack for the back. Use the handbag front and the handbag back for the quilt tops and muslin as each backing.

4 Adjust the sewing machine for straight-stitch quilting. Thread the needle with either brown or variegated quilting thread. Fill the bobbin with sewing thread. Stitch in the ditch of the pieced seams, and then stitch wavy or large zigzag rows in some of the open areas.

5 Press the bias-cut strip in half with wrong sides together so the long edges meet. Press the fold. Open out the strip so it's flat. Fold each raw edge to meet at the center crease. Press the folds. Fold the strip in half so the pressed folds meet. Press as you shape the strip into a curve to form the button loop. Stitch each long side through all layers. In the same way, fold and stitch the shoulder strap, but do not shape it into a curve.

6 Pin the button loop to one purple section to make the front flap (see figure 2). Adjust the size of the loop for the button you have selected, allowing for a ¹/₂-inch (1.3 cm) seam. Machine-baste the loop to the flap.

figure 2

7 Stack the front and back flaps with right sides together. Add the batting on top of the stack. Stitch the sides and loop-edge of the flap, using a ¹/₂-inch (1.3 cm) seam allowance and leaving the top edge of the flap open. Trim across the corners to reduce bulk. Turn the flap right side out.

8 Adjust the sewing machine for straight-stitch quilting. Thread the needle with variegated quilting thread. Topstitch ¹/₂ inch (1.3 cm) from the seamed edges of the flap, and then stitch large zigzags across the flap.

9 Attach the beads using either the hand-sewing or beading needle, depending upon the size of the bead hole. Thread the needle with beading thread. Identify the beading techniques by referring to figure 3. To begin, use a seed stitch to sew about eight topaz seed beads in the center of the flower motif on the front of the handbag; fill in the flower center with about 30 pewter seed beads. With the same stitch, sew about 12 bugle beads among the flower petals. Sew some scattered turquoise and yellow/lime seed beads on and around the flower.

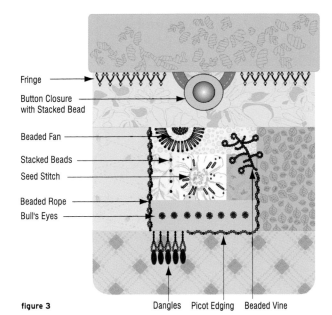

Fringe

Button Closure
with Stacked Bead

Beaded Fan

Stacked Beads

Seed Stitch

Beaded Rope

Bull's Eyes

figure 3

Dangles   Picot Edging   Beaded Vine

10 Sew a row of four sets of stacked beads to the left of the center flower. For each stack, sew a topaz seed bead on top of a size 8/0 purple seed bead.

11 Sew a row of eight bull's eyes below the center flower motif. For each bull's eye, sew a mustard marble seed bead in the center. Use a backstitch to sew a row of olive seed beads around the center. Thread the needle back through the first two beads to close the circle snugly (see figure 4). Add couching stitches as needed to make the row of beads lie snugly around the center bead.

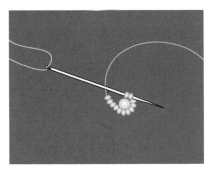

figure 4

12 Sew a beaded rope on the seam to the left of the stacked beads. Bring the thread out at one end of the seam. Pick up seven olive seed beads on the thread. Insert the needle at the seam, and pull the thread taut so the beads lay straight and snug. Bring the thread out between the third and fourth beads in the row (see figure 5). Pick up seven blackberry seed beads on the thread, and pull the thread taut so the blackberry beads begin to lie next to the olive beads and nudge the

olive beads slightly to one side. Insert the needle at the last blackberry bead and bring the thread out between the third and fourth blackberry beads (see figure 6). In the same way, continue sewing alternating bead colors to form the rope. For the final segment, you may have to use more or fewer beads to fill in the space.

figure 5   **figure 6**

13 Sew a picot edging using olive and blackberry seed beads along the seams that form the corner of the brown strip (see figure 7). Make a series of 11 picots.

figure 7

14 Sew a series of five dangles on the seam between the picot edging and the rope. For each dangle, string six size 11/0 purple seed beads, four olive seed beads, one teardrop bead, and four olive seed beads. Feed the needle back through the purple beads (see figure 8), and insert the needle through the handbag at the starting point. Pull the thread taut enough to bring the beads close together, but with enough slack so the dangle swings freely. Secure each dangle on the back with a knot.

figure 8

15 Sew a vine above the picot edging using orange seed beads for the branches and novelty beads with turquoise beads for the flowers. Use a backstitch about every three to five beads in each free-form vine segment. To sew each flower, stack a turquoise bead on a novelty bead.

16 Sew a beaded fan next to the vine. Use a bugle bead with a purple seed bead at one end and a blackberry seed bead at the other end to make each spoke. For the center of the fan, begin with a single size 8/0 purple seed bead in the center, then use a couching stitch to sew a strand of olive seed beads in a semi-circular row. In the same way, sew a second row of olive beads and then a row of turquoise beads.

17 Cut a 1-inch (2.5 cm) square from each bottom corner of the handbag front and back. With right sides together and using a 1/2-inch (1.3 cm) seam allowance, sew the front to the back along the sides and bottom (see figure 9). Press the seams open. In the same way, stitch the two lining sections together, but leave an opening in the bottom seam.

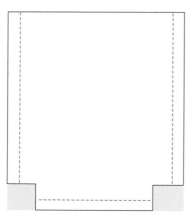

figure 9

18 Create the gusset at the bottom of the bag and lining by aligning the side and bottom seams at each corner. Stitch across each corner using a 1/2-inch (1.3 cm) seam allowance (see figure 10). Turn the handbag, but not the lining, right side out.

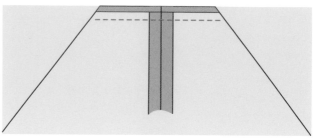

figure 10

19 Pin the shoulder strap to the handbag at each side seam (see figure 11). Machine-baste the ends of the strap to the handbag.

Side seam

figure 11

20 Pin the flap to the back of the handbag (see figure 12). Machine-baste the flap to the handbag, using a 1/2-inch (1.3 cm) seam allowance.

figure 12

DESIGNER
Note: The handbag strap may be cut from a single fabric or pieced from several fabrics.

21 Insert the handbag into the lining so the right sides are together. Align the lining and handbag so the side seams match. Sew a ¹/₂-inch (1.3 cm) seam around the top of the handbag. Turn the handbag right side out by pulling it through the opening in the lining's bottom seam. Close the opening with small hand stitches. Tack the corners of the lining to the corners of the bag by hand. Topstitch the seam around the top of the handbag.

22 Sew the button with the ¹/₂-inch (1.3 cm) bead on top to the handbag front below the button loop.

23 Sew a beaded fringe on the flap on each side of the button loop. Divide each space into eight equal parts and mark with chalk. Thread the beading needle with beading thread, and knot the end. Beginning at one side seam of the flap, insert the needle, pulling the thread until the knot pops through the seam. Bring the thread out at the edge of the flap; take one tiny stitch from back to front to secure the thread. For each segment of the fringe, pick up the following seed beads: one dark purple, one blue metallic, six purple, one mustard swirl, and one purple. Pass the needle over this last purple bead, through the mustard swirl bead and the next dark purple bead to pick up five dark purple, one blue, and one dark purple bead (see figure 13). At the edge of the flap, insert the needle from the

back through all layers of fabric to the front side of the flap. Take an additional small security stitch by bringing the needle and thread from the back to the front a few fabric threads' distance away. To begin the next fringe segment, insert the needle back through the dark purple and blue metallic beads (see figure 14) before repeating the pattern beginning with six purple beads. At the end of the fringe, take an additional small stitch. Make a knot in the thread, and pull the thread until the knot pops to the inside of the flap.

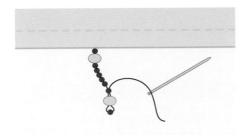

figure 13

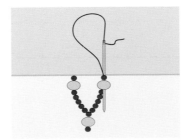

figure 14

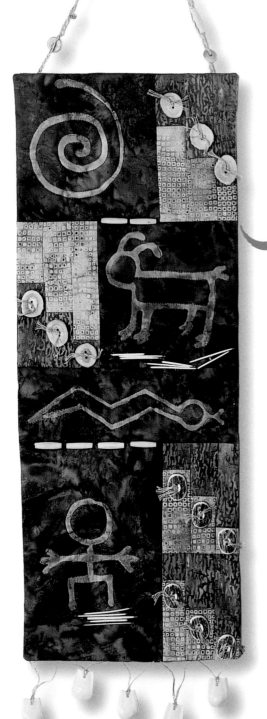

petroglyph
panel

Porcupine quills, elk's teeth beads, horn buttons, and jute twine are among the unexpected details that make this quilt unique. You can create the primitive fabric images with a discharge technique using common household products.

DESIGNER:
KATE GLEZEN CUTKO

FINISHED SIZE:
approximately 22 x 8 inches (55.9 x 20.3 cm)

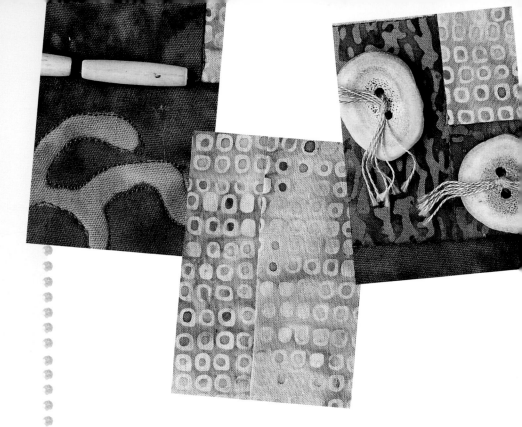

Materials

Quilt top and backing:
¾ yard (.7 m) of dark brown batik cotton fabric,
   44 inches (111.8 cm) wide
⅛ yard (.1 m) of medium brown print cotton fabric,
   44 inches (111.8 cm) wide
⅛ yard (.1 m) of light brown print cotton fabric,
   44 inches (111.8 cm) wide
Muslin fabric, 24 x 10 inches (61 x 25.4 cm)

Batting:
Low-loft cotton batting, 23 x 9 inches (58.4 x 22.9 cm)

Beads:
About 12 bone tube beads, 1 inch (2.5 cm) long
Six elk's tooth beads, 1 inch (2.5 cm) long
About 15 porcupine quills
12 horn buttons, ⅞ inch (2.2 cm) long
About 10 assorted small round and flat bone beads

Thread, etc:
Brown sewing thread
Brown 30 wt. cotton embroidery thread
Tan silk thread
Beige embroidery floss
Jute twine

Tools & Supplies

Chalk fabric marker
Bleach pen
Sink filled with warm water
Fine sandpaper
Small bowl of strong coffee
Embroidery needle with a large eye
Fray retardant
Jewelry glue
Wooden skewer
Craft knife

¼-inch (6 mm) seam allowance

1 Cut the following pieces from dark brown fabric
for the quilt top: two 6-inch (15.2 cm) squares,
one 4 x 9 inches (10.2 x 22.9 cm), and one 6 x 9 inches
(15.2 x 22.9 cm). Use the excess fabric to cut a 22 ½ x
8 ½-inch (57.2 x 21.6 cm) backing, and reserve.

2 Use the chalk marker to draw a spiral sun on
one square and a primitive elk on the other
square. Draw a simple snake on the 4 x 9-inch (10.2
x 22.9 cm) piece and a crude human figure on the
remaining piece. Trace the drawings with the bleach
pen. After five to eight minutes, rinse the pieces
thoroughly in a sink filled with warm water to stop
the bleaching process. Use a hot, dry iron to press the
fabric pieces until they are dry.

3 Cut twelve 6 x 1½-inch (15.2 x 3.8 cm) strips
each from the medium and light brown fabrics.

4 Adjust the sewing machine for straight
stitching. Thread the needle and fill the bobbin
with brown sewing thread. With right sides together,
sew the short end of each light brown strip to the
short end of a medium brown strip.

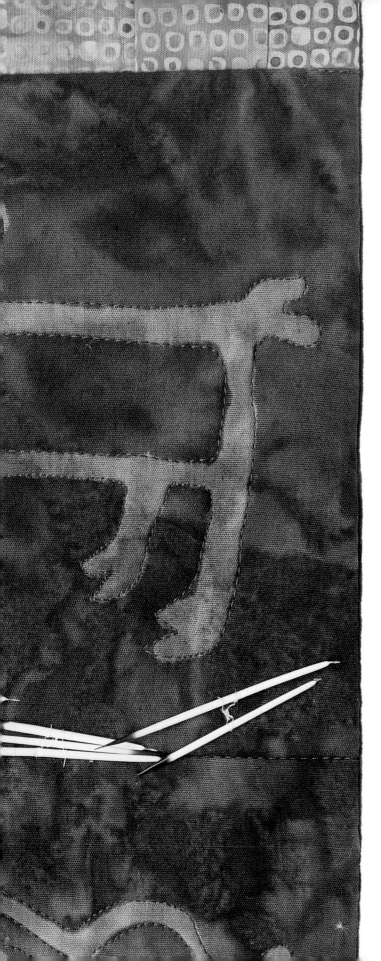

5   Divide the pieced strips into sets of three. Arrange each set so the seams are staggered by 1 inch (2.5 cm) like stair steps. Stitch the long sides of each set together (see figure 1).

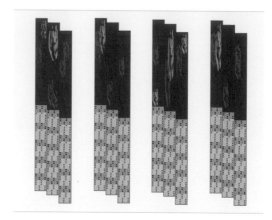

figure 1

6   Cut the following pieces from the pieced sets for the quilt top: two 3 ½ x 6 inches (8.9 cm x 15.2 cm) and two 3 ½ x 4 ½ inches (8.9 cm x 11.4 cm). Stitch the two smaller pieces together (see figure 2).

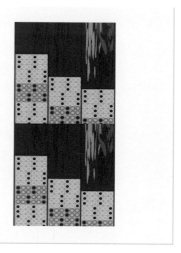

figure 2

DESIGNER Note: Test the bleach discharge process on scraps of the quilt top fabrics to preview the results. You'll notice that no two fabrics reveal the same color undertones after bleaching. To achieve images with the clarity you desire, you can adjust the elapsed bleaching time from as few as five to as many as eight minutes. If you prefer, substitute gel bleach cleanser for the bleach pen; pour the gel into a squeeze bottle that has a small applicator tip.

7 Arrange the quilt top pieces as shown in the photograph. Stitch the pieces together to form the quilt top.

8 Stack the quilt top, right side up; the batting; and the muslin. Baste the layers together with safety pins.

9 Adjust the sewing machine for free-motion quilting. Thread the needle with brown embroidery thread. Stitch around each of the bleached images on the quilt top. Stitch in the ditch of each of the seams.

10 Thread the embroidery needle with six strands of floss. Place a button next to each stepped seam by sewing floss through the quilt layers and the button's holes. Cut the ends of the floss, leaving long thread tails to tie in a knot. Trim the thread tails to 1 inch (2.5 cm). Secure each knot with a drop of fray retardant.

11 Arrange small clusters of quills under the image of the elk and the human. Adjust the sewing machine for a long straight stitch. Thread the needle with silk thread. Turn the machine's fly wheel slowly by hand to stitch back and forth over each cluster of quills three times; do not pierce the quills with the needle. Bring the thread tails to the muslin side. Apply glue to adhere the stitches to the quills on the quilt top. Let the glue dry.

12 Sand the surface of the tube beads lightly. Soak the beads in coffee overnight to darken them. Dry the beads. Using the embroidery needle threaded with six strands of floss, sew four beads over the seam below the snake image and two over the seam below the sun image.

13 Trim the quilt top to measure 22 1/2 x 8 1/2 inches (57.2 x 21.6 cm). Stack the backing and quilt top with right sides together. Sew around the edge, leaving an opening along the bottom seam. Trim the corners diagonally to reduce bulk. Turn the quilt right side out through the opening. Close the opening with small hand stitches.

14 Thread the embroidery needle with a long piece of twine. Sew five loops across the bottom of the quilt, threading an elk's tooth bead on each loop as you sew.

15 Trim the skewer to 7 inches (17.8 cm) long with the craft knife. Sew the skewer near the top edge of the backing with small hand stitches; place the stitches 1/2 inch (1.3 cm) in from each end of the skewer (see figure 3). Seal the stitches with a drop of fray retardant.

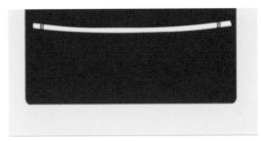

figure 3

16 Cut three pieces of twine, each about 20 inches (50.8 cm) long. Tie them together with an overhand knot in the center to form a hanging loop (see figure 4). On each side of the loop, braid the twine loosely and string the remaining bone beads randomly on the twine as you go. Tie each free end of the braid to one end of the skewer with a knot. Seal each knot with a drop of fray retardant.

figure 4

seaweed
purse

Build up a texture as rich as the bottom of the sea with layers of sheer fabrics, novelty yarns, shells, and beads of all sizes. Turn flat pebbles into beads with a tulle wrap, and roll the tube beads from strips of lamé fabric.

DESIGNER:

JULIA DONALDSON

FINISHED SIZE:
approximately 13 ½ x 7 inches (34.3 x 17.8 cm)

Materials

Purse front and back:

⅜ yard (.3 m) of dark blue cotton fabric, 44 inches (111.8 cm) wide

⅛ yard (.1 m) each of two shades of brown sheer polyester fabric such as organza or organdy, 60 inches (152.4 cm) wide

¼ yard (.2 m) of green polyester lining fabric, 45 inches (114.3 cm) wide

⅛ yard (.1 m) of gold tulle netting, 54 inches (137.2 cm) wide

Purse lining:

¼ yard (.2 m) of green cotton fabric, 44 inches (111.8 cm) wide

Beads:

About 1,000 assorted beads in brown, gold, and green, sized from small seed beads to large beads about ½ inch (1.3 cm) in diameter

About 15 white seashell beads, ½ to 1 inch (1.3 to 2.5 cm)

Copper cotton/nylon lamé fabric, 10 x 15 inches (25.4 x 38.1 cm)

Fusible web, 10 x 15 inches (25.4 x 38.1 cm)

About 12 small, flat pebbles

Batting:

Low-loft batting, 24 x 10 inches (61 x 25.4 cm)

Thread, etc:

Brown polyester machine embroidery thread

Assorted brown and gold novelty yarns

Green cotton sewing thread

Brown polyester sewing thread

Two pieces of driftwood, about 8 inches (20.3 cm) long and ½ to ¾ inch (1.3 to 1.9 cm) in diameter

Tools & Supplies

Metallic gold acrylic paint

Small paintbrush

Wax paper

Evaporating ink fabric marker

Candle

Match

Heat-resistant saucer

Embroidery needle with a large eye

Small hand-sewing needle for beading

Metal knitting needle

¼-inch (6 mm) seam allowance

1   Lay the shell beads on wax paper. Paint the shells, and let them dry.

2   Wrap each flat pebble in a square of tulle large enough to twist into a 1½- to 2-inch (3.8 to 5 cm) tail. Take several hand stitches through the tail to secure the tulle snugly around the pebble. Wrap the thread around the tail several times, and then take several stitches through the tail to secure the thread. Trim the tail to about ⅛ inch (3 mm).

3   Follow the manufacturer's directions to apply the fusible web to the wrong side of the lamé. Cut the lamé into 1-inch (2.5 cm) strips, and then cut the strips into 1½-inch (3.8 cm) lengths to create 75 strips measuring 1 x 1½-inches (2.5 x 3.8 cm). To make each lamé bead, lay a strip, fusible side up on the work surface. Beginning at a short end, roll the strip tightly around the knitting needle. Press to fuse the lamé layers together. Slide the bead off the needle.

4   Mark three 2 x 23-inch (5 x 58.4 cm) overlay strips on each of the brown organza or organdy fabrics and twelve 18 x ¾ to 1-inch (45.7 x 1.9 to 2.5 cm) fringe strips on the green lining fabric. Use scissors to cut out the strips roughly for an organic look. Also mark four 9 x 2½-inch (22.9 x 6.4 cm) strips on the brown fabric; cut out these cleanly with a rotary cutter, and reserve for the handle straps. Also mark two 11 x 8-inch (27.9 x 20.3 cm) sections on the green fabric; cut out these cleanly, and reserve for the purse lining.

For safety's sake, heat-seal the polyester strips for the fringe while working outdoors or in a well-ventilated room. You may also want to wear a respirator for this step, and use pliers or tongs to handle the strips.

5 Stand the candle in the saucer, and light the wick. Heat-seal each overlay, fringe, and handle strip by holding it taut and slightly above the flame. Move the strip slowly to melt the fibers along each raw edge (see figure 1).

figure 1

6 Cut a 23 x 9-inch (58.4 x 22.9 cm) purse front/ back from the blue fabric. Also cut four 2 1/2 x 8 1/2-inch (6.4 x 21.6 cm) strips and reserve for the handle straps.

7 Stack the batting and the purse front/back section, right side up, so an equal margin of batting extends all around. Baste the layers together. Arrange the brown overlay strips so they completely cover the purse front/back fabric. Pin the strips in place. Adjust the sewing machine for straight stitching. Thread the needle and fill the bobbin with embroidery thread. Stitch along each edge of each strip. Trim the purse front/back to measure 22 x 8 inches (55.9 x 20.3 cm). Use a long straight stitch to baste the strips to the seam allowance along the edges.

8 Fold the purse front/back with the shorter edges aligned. Mark the fold; this is the bottom of the purse. The shorter edges are the top of the purse.

9 Thread the embroidery needle with about 20 inches (50.8 cm) of a novelty yarn, and make a knot 4 inches (10.2 cm) from the end. Beginning at the bottom of the purse, sew large running stitches in a meandering row toward the top of the purse. Do not sew the yarn within the seam allowances. Let the 4 inches (10.2 cm) of yarn below the knot hang freely as fringe. At the top, secure the yarn with a knot on the batting side. Thread the needle with another novelty yarn, and stitch in the same way. Repeat eight to 10 times on each half of the purse, front and back, spacing the rows of stitches about 1/2 inch (1.3 cm) apart.

10 Pin each green fringe strip on the purse so one end aligns with one of the top edges of the purse and the excess floats freely beyond the bottom of the purse (see figure 2). Stagger the strips, twist them loosely, and overlap them to look like seaweed. Place them next to, but not within, the seam allowances on the long side edges of the purse. Leave an irregular area about 1 1/2 to 2 inches (3.8 to 5 cm) wide along the center of the purse free for beading. Use hand stitches to tack one long edge of each strip to the purse.

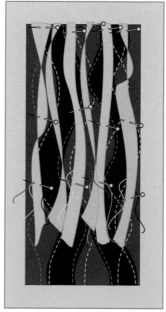

figure 2

" I hang my decorative purses on the wall as works of art just as I would a wall quilt. I can take them down and use them for special occasions. – JULIA DONALDSON, DESIGNER "

11 Arrange the lamé beads on the purse between the green fringe strips. Orient the beads vertically, and do not place them within the seam allowances. Thread the needle with polyester thread and sew along the center back of each bead to secure it to the purse.

12 Thread the needle with polyester thread. Sew seed beads in a scattered arrangement along the outline of the free center area on the purse. Sew the shell beads, other larger beads, and flat pebbles to the center area. Fill in the spaces around the pebbles, shells, and larger beads with assorted smaller beads. Do not sew any beads within the seam allowances.

13 Fold the purse in half along the bottom mark with right sides together. Sew the side seams. Turn the purse right side out. Press the seams to one side.

14 Stack two brown strips on the right side of each blue strip for the handle straps. Sew along the edges by machine. Trim the brown strips even with the blue fabric. Fold each strip in half with right sides together so it measures 8 x 1¼ inches (20.3 x 3.2 cm); sew the seam across one short end and down the long side. Turn each strap right side out. Press. Fold each strap in half so it measures 3 ¾ x 1 inch (9.5 x 2.5 cm). Baste the raw edges of the straps to the top edge of the purse (see figure 3).

15 Sew the lining side seams with right sides together. Leave the top and bottom of the lining open.

16 Slide the purse, right side out, into the lining, wrong side out. Match the purse and lining at the side seams and the top edges. Sew the seam around the top of the purse.

17 Turn the lining right side out by bringing it up and over the purse. Turn under the seam allowances at the bottom of the lining. Pin the seam, and topstitch.

18 Push the lining inside the purse. Press the seam at the top of the purse. Topstitch this seam close to the folded edge.

19 Insert the driftwood handles into the handle straps. Sew the handle strap edges together by hand below the handles (see figure 4).

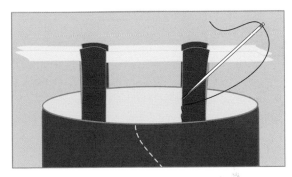

figure 4

figure 3

horror
VACUI

The title of this quilt describes its style—a surface filled with images, decorative shapes, and ornamental details. Row upon row of glittering gold bugle beads leave very little visible of the gold silk fabric used for the quilt top.

DESIGNER:
JENNIFER A. REIS

FINISHED SIZE:
approximately 12 x 7 ½ inches
(30.5 x 19 cm)

Materials

Quilt top:
Gold silk dupioni fabric, 12 x 7 ½ inches (30.5 x 19 cm)

Appliqués:
Red print cotton or cotton blend fabric, 14 x 9 ½ inches (35.6 x 24.1 cm)
Off-white polyester/cotton blend damask fabric, 4 x 2 ½ inches (10.2 x 6.4 cm)

Backing:
Pink skull print cotton fabric, 12 x 7 ½ inches (30.5 x 19 cm)

Batting:
Low-loft polyester batting, 12 x 7 ½ inches (30.5 x 19 cm)

Beads:
Two costume jewelry earrings with any clip backs removed
1 x 1 ½-inch (2.5 x 3.8 cm) metallic silver breastplate pendant
¾ x 1-inch (1.9 x 2.5 cm) metallic silver medal pendant
Two wooden beads 1 inch (2.5 cm) in diameter with side-drilled holes and saint images
Two silver pailette sequins, 1 inch (2.5 cm) in diameter
One hank (about 860) size 3 silver-lined gold bugle beads
About 48 seed beads

Thread, etc:
Two to three skeins of dark purple embroidery floss
Off-white sewing thread
Gray upholstery thread
7 inches (17.8 cm) of sew-on hook-and-loop tape
Shrink polymer plastic sheet, 2 x 3 ½ inches (5 x 8.9 cm)

Tools & Supplies

Freezer paper
Pencil
Embroidery needle with a large eye
Hand-sewing needle
Beading needle
Hole punch
Fine-point pen with permanent black ink
Staple gun

Templates

See page 125

Instructions

1 Trace the templates for the skull and frame onto the matte side of freezer paper to make the appliqué patterns.

2 Press the skull pattern, shiny side down, on the right side of the damask fabric. In the same way, press the frame pattern on the red print fabric. Cut out the appliqués on the traced lines. Remove the freezer paper patterns.

3 Stack and baste the quilt layers. Fold under the raw edges of the frame appliqué ½ inch (1.3 cm) where marked on the template, and press. Place the frame appliqué on the quilt top with the edges of all the layers aligned. Pin the appliqué to the quilt top.

4 Thread the embroidery needle with two strands of floss. Sew a buttonhole stitch through all the quilt layers around the outside edge, spacing the stitches about ⅛ inch (3 mm) apart. In the same way, stitch around the raw edges of the appliqué.

5 Thread the hand-sewing needle with off-white sewing thread. Pin the skull appliqué in the center of the large opening of the frame appliqué. Sew the skull appliqué with very small buttonhole stitches, sewing through all the quilt layers.

> " Utilizing symbolism in appliqué is an effective way for me to communicate narrative through textile art. When I'm researching a new piece, I often look to examples from art history that fit my aesthetic. "
> – JENNIFER REIS, DESIGNER

6 Thread the needle with upholstery thread. Referring to the photograph for placement, sew the earrings, pendants, and wooden beads to the quilt.

7 Thread the embroidery needle with six strands of floss. Place a pailette sequin in the frame appliqué opening at each lower corner of the quilt. Sew four large stitches across each sequin to form a net (see figure 1). Sew closely spaced buttonhole stitches to partially enclose each sequin; form the stitches between the edge of the sequin and the net (see figure 2).

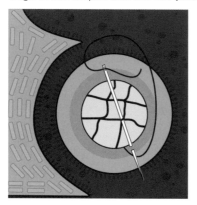

figure 1

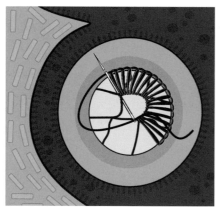

figure 2

8 Thread the beading needle with upholstery thread. Sew a row of seed beads next to the buttonhole stitches around each sequin.

9 Use the beading needle and upholstery thread to sew bugle beads end-to-end to outline each frame opening on the top half of the quilt, the large center opening, and the skull appliqué. Sew the stitches through all the quilt layers. In the same way, sew a radiating row of bugle beads around each wooden bead. Fill in the remaining spaces with bugle beads sewn end-to-end in rows that echo the shape of the outline rows.

10 Punch a hole near each corner of the piece of shrink plastic. Use the pen to write your name, the title of the quilt, the date, and any other information you would like to include on the label. Follow the manufacturer's directions to process the shrink plastic. Sew the label to the quilt backing.

11 Sew the loop half of the hook-and-loop tape to the top of the quilt backing. Staple the hook half to the wall. Press the halves of the tape together to hang the quilt.

DESIGNER *Note:* The dense field of gold bugle beads in the center of the quilt offers an opportunity to embed additional, subtle images on the quilt such as a pair of snakes surrounding the skull appliqué. To add this detail, use basting stitches to outline each image. Sew a row of bugle beads end-to-end along the basted outline, and then remove the basting stitches. Fill in the image with rows of beads that echo the shape of the outline row.

pomegranate
book cover

Beautifully quilted with free-motion stitching, this soft cover with beaded
appliqués transforms an ordinary school supply into an elegant blank book
suitable for a special use, perhaps as a journal or a keepsake guest registry.
The cover can be made either with a vertical or a horizontal orientation.

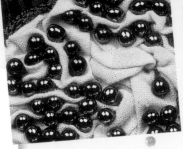

DESIGNER:
SARAH ANN SMITH

FINISHED SIZE:
10 x 7 inch (25.4 x 17.8 cm)

Materials

Quilt top:
Lime-green batik cotton fabric, 7 x 30 ½ inches (17.8 x 77.5 cm)
Turquoise batik cotton fabric, 4 x 30 ½ inches (10.2 x 77.5 cm)

Backing:
Muslin fabric, 12 x 18 inches (30.5 x 45.7 cm)

Batting:
Low-loft batting, 12 x 18 inches (30.5 x 45.7 cm)

Lining:
Red print fabric, 10 ¾ x 6 ½ inches (27.3 x 16.5 cm)

Thread, etc:
Lime-green and brown 40 wt. polyester machine embroidery thread
Tan 60 wt. polyester machine embroidery thread

Beads:
About 300 red teardrop beads

Appliqués:
3 red print cotton fabrics blending from light to dark, a 6-inch
   (15.2 cm) square of each
White cotton fabric, 6 x 12 inches (15.2 x 30.5 cm)
Fusible interfacing, 4 x 8 inches (10.2 x 20.3 cm)
¼ yard (.2 m) of lightweight fusible web, 20 inches (50.8 cm) wide

Thread, etc:
Cranberry and pink 40 wt. polyester quilting thread
Tan 60 wt. polyester quilting thread
Clear monofilament beading thread

Tools & Supplies

Chalk fabric marker
Freezer paper
Pencil
Parchment paper
Spray bottle of water
Sheet of plastic
Paintbrush
Yellow, fuchsia, and red transparent fabric paint
Plastic plate
Water
Small hand-sewing needle for beading
Point turner

Templates

See page 121

½-inch (1.3 cm) seam allowance

DESIGNER *Note:*

When free-motion quilting, use
a fill pattern around motifs such
as leaves or vines to raise them
slightly. Select regular 40 wt.
machine embroidery thread to quilt
the main motifs, and then switch to
the finer 60 wt. thread for the more
closely spaced fill stitches.

Instructions

1 Sew the two quilt top fabric pieces together. Press the seam allowance toward the smaller fabric section (this section will become the lower part of the finished cover).

2 Fold under ¹/₂ inch (1.3 cm) on each side edge for a hem. Stitch ³/₈ inch (9.5 mm) from each fold.

3 Fold the quilt top in half so the side edges meet. Mark the center along the fold.

4 Stack the quilt top, right side down; the batting, centered; and the muslin backing, centered over the batting. Baste with safety pins.

5 Adjust the sewing machine for free-motion quilting. Thread the needle with 40 wt. embroidery thread to match the fabric. Fill the bobbin with 60 wt. thread. Stitch a different design on each of the two fabrics on the quilt top; for example, stitch diamonds with crosshatching, a diagonal wood-grain pattern, or a vine design.

6 Place two drops of yellow, two drops of red, and four to six drops of fuchsia paint on the plastic plate. Mix the fuchsia and red paints together, and dilute the mixture with water until it is very thin. Likewise, dilute the yellow paint with water.

7 Place the white cotton fabric on the plastic sheet. Spray the fabric with water until damp. Brush the red/fuchsia paint mixture on the fabric to paint it a very pale pink color. Brush the yellow paint here and there over the pink paint to turn the fabric a soft variegated peach color. Let the paints dry. Follow the paint manufacturer's directions to heat-set the colors.

As an optional detail, make an extra small pomegranate appliqué for the back of the book cover. Use plain, flat fabric for the contrast, and substitute embroidery for the beads so the book rests flat.

8 Place the painted fabric on a parchment sheet. Spray the fabric with water until damp. Scrunch the fabric, creating little nooks and crannies, until it measures about 4 x 8 inches (10.2 x 20.3 cm). Follow the manufacturer's directions to fuse interfacing on the scrunched fabric. Press from both sides to set the fabric texture.

9 Trace the templates onto the matte side of freezer paper to make appliqué patterns. Follow the manufacturer's directions to apply fusible web to the wrong side of the three red fabrics. Place the pomegranate patterns, shiny side down, on the right side of the red fabrics and the contrast patterns, shiny side down, on the scrunched fabric. Press the patterns to hold them temporarily on the fabrics. Cut out the appliqués. Remove the patterns.

10 Assemble each pomegranate appliqué on a parchment sheet. Overlap the appliqué sections where indicated on the patterns. Cover the appliqués with a parchment sheet, and press.

11 Wrap the cover around the closed book. Fold the hem ends inside the book covers. Mark where the cover falls on the side, top, and bottom edges of the book. Arrange the pomegranate appliqués on the front cover, and pin in place.

12 Remove the cover from the book. Open the cover out flat. Remove the pins from the appliqués. Fuse the appliqués in place.

13 Adjust the sewing machine for zigzag stitching, choosing a medium stitch width and a short stitch length, or adjust the sewing machine for straight stitching, choosing a short stitch length. Stitch the raw edges of the appliqués, matching the thread color to the lighter and darker red fabrics. Use tan thread to stitch the scrunched contrast appliqués.

14 Thread the needle with beading thread. Sew beads individually using a seed stitch, nestling them into the scrunched folds of the contrast appliqués. At times pick up two or three beads with one stitch. Sew some individual beads below the pomegranate appliqués.

15 Wrap the cover around the book to test the fit. Check the accuracy of the markings for the center of the spine. Use chalk to mark the side, top, and bottom edges of the book. Remove the cover from the book.

16 Apply fusible web to the wrong side of the lining.

17 Place the cover right side up. Fold the hemmed edges back at the sides. Center the lining right side down over the spine (see figure 1). Sew the seam across the top and bottom of the cover. Turn the cover right side out and test the fit; if necessary, sew a deeper or narrower seam. Trim the seam allowances to $1/2$ inch (1.3 cm). Press the seams as sewn.

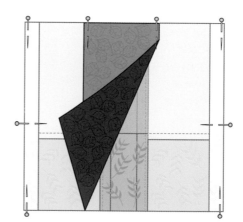

figure 1

18 Turn the cover right side out. Use a point turner tool to help the corners to turn completely.

19 Fuse the lining in place.

20 Slide the book into the cover.

I've been working on a series of small projects based on a book about reputedly aphrodisiac foods. Pomegranates are among those foods, plus they taste good, look good, and often serve as a symbol for women.
– SARAH ANN SMITH, DESIGNER ”

reach for the *stars*

Combine two
fascinating beading
techniques to create
the rich texture
on this quilt. Use
massed strands of
beads for the flowing
hair, and nestle
rows of single beads
among the swirling
floss spirals.

DESIGNER:
SUE SPURLOCK

FINISHED SIZE:
approximately 16 x 11 inches (40.6 x 27.9 cm)

Materials

Quilt top, appliqués, hanging sleeve, and binding:
Fat quarter of turquoise batik cotton fabric
Rose/purple batik cotton fabric, 6 ½ x 10 inches (16.5 x 25.4cm)
Blue/purple batik cotton fabric, 3 x 4 inches (7.6 x 10.2 cm)
Crisp woven cotton fusible interfacing, 13 x 25 inches (33 x 63.5 cm)

Batting:
Low-loft batting, 18 x 13 inches (45.7 x 33 cm)

Beads:
Glass seed beads in size 10/0 or 11/0: about 2,200 (10 grams) of silver-lined turquoise; about 4,400 (20 grams) of silver-lined silver; about 220 (1 gram) of metallic pink; and about 880 (4 grams) of multicolored red/pink
About 20 opalescent star beads

Backing:
Batik cotton fabric, 19 x 14 inches (48.3 x 35.6 cm)

Threads, etc:
Turquoise, red, and dark blue sewing thread
2 skeins each of light, medium, and dark turquoise embroidery floss
1 skein of rose embroidery floss

Tools & Supplies

Pencil
Tracing paper
Small hand-sewing needle for beading
Embroidery needle with a large eye
Beading needle

Templates

See page 120

¼-inch (6 mm) seam allowance unless noted otherwise

Instructions

1 From the fat quarter of fabric, cut an 18 x 13-inch (45.7 x 33 cm) quilt top. Also cut four 1½ x 18-inch (3.8 x 45.7 cm) binding strips and a 4½ x 10-inch (11.4 x 25.4 cm) hanging sleeve, and reserve for the finishing steps.

2 Follow the manufacturer's directions to fuse interfacing to the wrong side of the quilt top. Reserve the remaining interfacing for the appliqués.

3 Use a pencil to mark the quilt top 2 inches (5.1 cm) in from the edges as a guide for the finished size of the quilt (the pencil marks will be covered with binding during the finishing step). Fold the quilt top on the marked lines, and press the folds to crease-mark the outline of the finished quilt.

> Just as a painter adds different colors of paint, quilting the spirals and shapes around the figure adds more depth, movement, and texture. I love the feel of using my hands and being so intimately inside the process. "
>
> – SUE SPURLOCK, DESIGNER

4 Trace the circle template onto tracing paper. Cut out the template. Use the template and a pencil to mark large spirals in a free-form arrangement on the quilt top. For the outer edge of each spiral, trace three-fourths of the way around the template, then remove the template to draw the inner spiral freehand (see figure 1). Swirl some of the spirals clockwise and others counterclockwise. Mark smaller spirals freehand between the large spirals, overlapping some of the large spirals as you mark. Mark an X in the center of each spiral for the placement of each star bead.

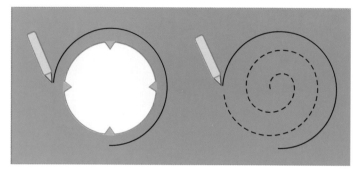

figure 1

5 Trace the appliqué templates onto the smooth side of the fusible interfacing. Cut out each template.

6 Follow the manufacturer's directions to fuse the cutout torso interfacing piece to the wrong side of the blue/purple fabric. Fuse the remaining interfacing pieces to the wrong side of the rose/purple fabric. Cut out each appliqué 1/4 inch (6 mm) from the edge of the interfacing (see figure 2).

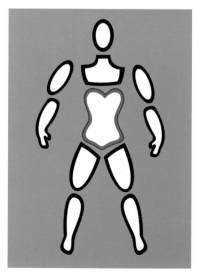

figure 2

7 Use a pencil to mark a spiral on each breast area of the torso appliqué, swirling the spirals in opposite directions. Mark a spiral at the hip area of the torso appliqué.

8 Arrange the appliqués on the quilt top. Place the head about 3 inches (7.6 cm) below the center of the upper creased line. Note that some of the appliqués will cover the marked spirals.

9 Fold the seam allowance to the wrong side of each appliqué except where the appliqués overlap, such as where the head meets the neck and where the legs meet the torso. Where the appliqués overlap, fold under the seam allowance on the overlapping layer only; the layer underneath should remain flat and unfolded to minimize bulk. Clip the seam allowances where necessary so they lie flat. Use your fingers to crease along the folded edges. Use fabric glue to hold the seam allowances in place and to baste the appliqués to the quilt top.

10 Sew the appliqué pieces in place with small hand stitches.

11 Press the quilt top so the appliquéd figure is flat. Thread the embroidery needle with three strands of rose floss. Use a stem stitch to embroider the spirals on the torso.

12 Thread the hand-sewing needle with turquoise thread. Couch six strands of medium turquoise floss all around the appliquéd figure.

13 Thread the embroidery needle with six strands of floss. Embroider the spirals on the quilt top with a stem stitch. Choose light, medium, or dark turquoise floss for each spiral.

14 Press the quilt top, right side down.

15 Stack the quilt top, right side up, on the batting. Baste the layers together with safety pins.

16 Thread the sewing needle with turquoise thread, and double the thread. For each spiral, begin by sewing a star bead in the center. As you continue to sew around the spiral, sew a silver-lined silver bead about every 1/8 inch (3 mm). In the same way, sew silver-lined turquoise beads around the outside of each spiral.

17 Thread the needle with red thread, and double the thread. Sew pink beads a scant 1/16 inch (1.5 mm) apart along the spirals on the torso.

18 Thread the beading needle with red thread, and double the thread. About an inch (2.5 cm) above the head, secure the thread by bringing the needle out, looping the thread into a knot, and inserting the needle back under the head (see figure 3). Bring the needle out at the hairline in the center of the head to start. String about 3 inches (7.6 cm) of multicolored red/pink beads on the thread for each strand of hair. Bring the needle over the end bead and back through the string of beads (see figure 4). Insert the needle at the hairline, and bring it out at the top of the head. Make a small knot in the thread (the knot will be covered later with beads). Continue sewing strands of beads around the head.

figure 4

20 Stack the beaded quilt top, right side up, on the wrong side of the backing. Baste the layers together. Thread the hand-sewing needle with turquoise thread. Use running stitches to quilt each spiral between the couched floss and the row of beads.

21 Press the quilt, right side down.

22 Bind the quilt, using a 1/2-inch (1.3 cm) seam allowance and mitered corners.

23 Thread the hand-sewing needle with red thread. Couch six strands of rose floss to the quilt top along the binding seam.

24 Sew the hanging sleeve to the backing.

figure 3

19 Arrange the strands of beads to look like a flowing head of hair. Couch each strand in place.

DESIGNER Note: If you find that the extensive hand embroidery distorts the quilt top, restore the shape by spraying it with water to dampen it. Pull the edges until they are straight and square, and pin the quilt top to a padded surface until dry.

gallery

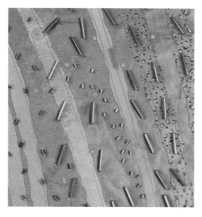

Alison Muir
Bush Regeneration, 2003–2005
60 x 49 x ¼ inches
(152.4 x 124.5 x 0.6 cm)
Commercial silks, polyester,
cotton, paint; fused appliqué,
beaded, machine quilted,
refinished; glass beads
Photos by Andrew Payne, Photographix

Patti Shaw
Mother of God Icon III, 2001
44 x 37 ½ inches (112 x 95.3 cm)
Cotton, found objects, paint;
appliqué, photo transferred, hand
quilted; seed beads, sequins
Photos by Mark Frey
Private collection

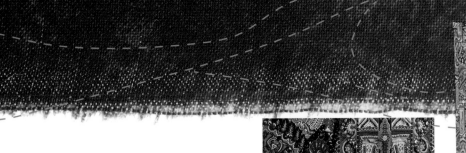

Patti Shaw
Queen of Heaven II, 2002
69 x 34 ¼ inches
(175.3 x 87 cm)
Commercial cotton fabric;
photo transferred, hand quilted;
seed beads, sequins
Photos by Mark Frey
Private collection

Lisa Binkley
Between the Woods and Frozen Lake, 2007
12 x 18 x ¼ inches (30.5 x 45.7 x 0.6 cm)
Cotton, nylon, polyester; machine appliqué
and quilted, hand beaded; glass, pearl, and
ceramic beads
Photos by Jim Couee
Collection of the University of Wisconsin
Children's Hospital

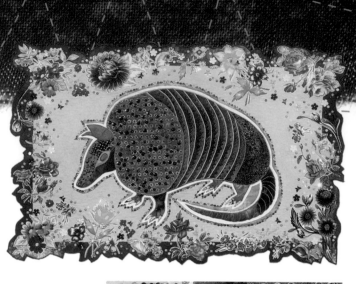

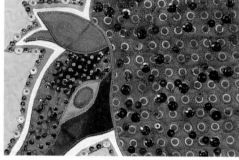

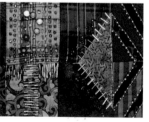

Sally A. Sellers
A Stitch in Time, 2002
39 x 26 x ½ inches (99 x 66 x 1.3 cm)
Cotton, silk; machine pieced and quilted, hand embroidered and beaded; glass and plastic beads
Photos by Bill Bachhuber
Collection of Multnomah County, Oregon

Betsy Cannon
Amarillo Armadillo, 2007
24 x 36 inches (61 x 91.4 cm)
Cotton, oil cloth, paint, sequins; machine appliqué and quilted, stamped; glass beads
Photos by Marcia Ward

Sally A. Sellers
When We Think about Spring, 2006
25 ½ x 35 ½ x ¼ inches
(64.8 x 90.2 x 0.6 cm)
Cotton; machine appliqué, hand embroidered and beaded; glass and crystal beads
Photos by artist

Betsy Cannon
Don't Fence Me In, Baby!, 2007
24 x 24 inches (61 x 61 cm)
Cotton, oil cloth, paint, ribbon; machine
and hand appliqué, machine quilted, photo
transferred; glass beads, buttons, sequins,
metal charms
Photos by Marcia Ward

Great Lakes Beadworkers Guild
*Great Lakes Beadworkers Guild Memorial
Quilt for Barb Davis*, 2006
22 x 40 inches (56 x 102 cm)
Interfacing; hand beaded; Japanese and
Czech beads, pearls, semiprecious stones,
vintage and lampworked beads
Photos by Tim Thayer

Judi Goolsby
Modern Maya: San Juan Chamula, 2005
48 x 36 inches (122 x 91.4 cm)
Cotton velveteen, paint; hand and over
dyed, silk-screened, stamped, machine
quilted, hand quilted, embroidered,
appliqué, and beaded; size 11° glass beads
Photos by artist

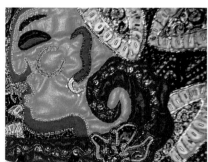

Susan R. Sorrell
Hurricane Jazz, 2002
17 ¹/₂ x 23 inches
(44.5 x 58.4 cm)
Cotton, batting, fabric
paint, embellishments;
hand quilted and
embroidered; glass beads
Photos by Rodney Sorrell

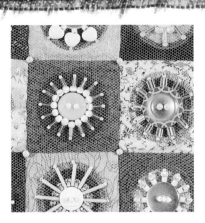

Therese Bliss
The Promise of Spring, 2006
20 x 16 inches (50.8 x 40.6 cm)
Cotton fabric, nylon netting; machine
pieced and quilted, fused, satin stitched;
buttons, glass beads
Photos by Robert Sherwood

Marilyn Gillis
Genesis, 2005
28 x 22 inches (71 x 56 cm)
Hand-made silk paper, cotton fabric;
machine pieced and quilted; glass beads
Photos by James Barbour

Faye Anderson
Old Year/New Year I, 1995
23 x 23 inches (58.4 x 58.4 cm)
Cotton; hand appliqué and
quilted, machine pieced; glass
beads, buttons, metallic charms
Photos by Ken Sanville

Do Palma
Platonic Vegetables, 2004
18 x 18 inches (45.7 x 45.7 cm)
Cotton fabrics, cotton and
rayon thread; machine pieced
and appliqué, hand beaded;
glass seed beads
Photos by artist

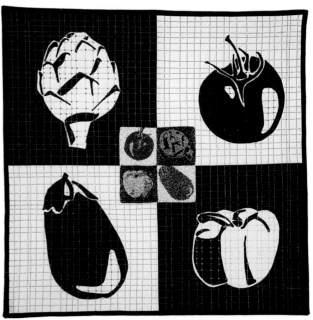

Susan Shie
Peace Cupboard, 2004
16 x 21 inches (40.6 x 53.3 cm)
Cotton, fabric paint; whole-
cloth brush painted, written,
hand embroidered and quilted;
glass beads
Photos by artist

Ellie Beth Scott
Special Dress, 2004
28 x 18 inches (71 x 45.7 cm)
Cotton, fabric, paint; hand
sewn; beads, buttons
Photos by artist

Susan Shie
Flight of the Art Angels, 2003
18 x 25 ¹⁄₂ inches (45.7 x 64.8 cm)
Cotton, fabric paint; whole-cloth brush
painted, written, hand embroidered
and quilted; glass beads
Photos by artist

Charlotte Kruk n' Kempken
*An Even Exchange and I Left You Some Change Tooth
Fairy 2000 (*From the documentary series *Pin-Ups &
Paper Dolls*), 2000–2007
13 ¹⁄₂ x 17 x ¹⁄₂ inches (34.3 x 43.2 x 1.3 cm)
Quilted cloth diaper, teeth cleaning products, tooth,
paint, coins; hand embroidered, machine appliqué; glass
seed beads, bugle beads
Photos by Keay Edwards

Lisa Binkley
Going In, 2006
15 x 15 x $\frac{1}{2}$ inches
(38 x 38 x 1.3 cm)
Cotton fabrics, hand-dyed cotton
and silk thread, polyester and
nylon thread; machine pieced
and embroidered, hand beaded,
embroidered, and quilted; glass,
pearl, ceramic, and stone beads
Photos by artist

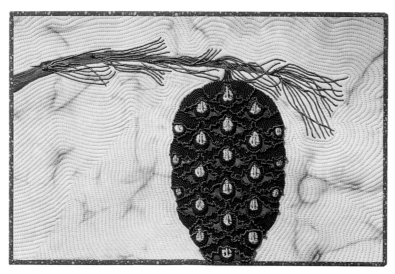

Casey Puetz
Keiko Study #1, 2005
22 $\frac{1}{4}$ x 20 $\frac{3}{4}$ inches (56.5 x 52.7 cm)
Commercial batik cotton, monofilament,
rayon thread, hand-dyed pearl cotton;
machine and hand quilted, embellished;
glass seed beads, bugle beads
Photos by artist

1023/1023a
Carol Krueger
Happy Trails, 2003
47 x 41 inches (119.4 x 104 cm)
Commercial cotton denim, cotton prints
and welt, silver conchos; machine pieced
and quilted, direct appliqué; seed beads,
Japanese delica beads
Photos by artist
Collection of Vikki Stevens

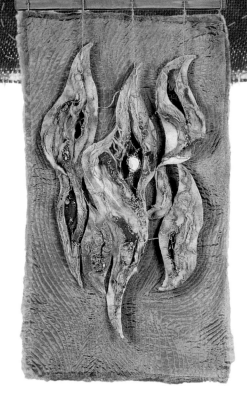

Marilyn Gillis
Flowers and Brambles, 2005
21 x 23 inches (53.3 x 58.4 cm)
Cotton fabric; machine embroidered and quilted,
hand embroidered; glass beads
Photos by James Barbour

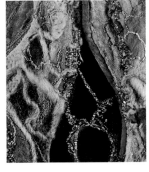

Martine House
*Un Autre Monde (Another
World)*, 2005
48 x 26 inches (122 x 66 cm)
Hand-dyed cotton velveteen
and silk, hand-dyed and
commercial fabrics, synthetic
fabrics; hand embroidered
and quilted, needle
felted, couched, beaded,
embellished; various glass
beads, dyed agate
Photos by Tim Barnwell

Do Palma
Rizpah, 2003
22 x 22 inches (55.9 x 55.9 cm)
Hand-dyed cotton fabrics,
cotton velveteen, silver lamé,
metallic foils, fabric paints,
metallic, rayon, and cotton
threads; hand foiled and
beaded, silk-screened, machine
appliqué and quilted; glass
seed beads
Photos by artist

Michele Schaefer-Parr
Return to Dust, 2006
12 x 7 ¹/₂ inches (30.5 x 19 cm)
Fabric, bone, paper, found objects;
sewn, painted, beaded
Photos by Lark Books

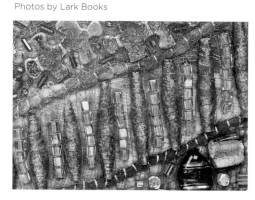

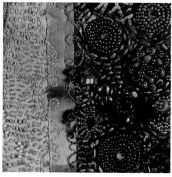

Lisa Binkley
Seedlings, 2007
12 x 18 x ¹/₂ inches (30.5 x 45.7 x 1.3 cm)
Cotton, rayon, and nylon thread;
machine appliqué and quilted, hand
beaded; glass and ceramic beads
Photos by Edward Binkley
Collection of the University of Wisconsin
Children's Hospital

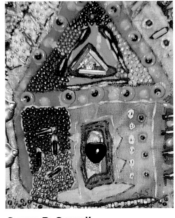

Susan R. Sorrell
The Hard Truth about Dreams, 2003
8 x 7 ¼ inches (20.3 x 18.4 cm)
Cotton, fabric paint, batting,
embellishments; machine and hand
quilted, hand embroidered; glass beads
Photos by Rodney Sorrell

Randy Frost
Out of Line, 2004
9 ⁷/₈ x 6 ½ inches (25 x 16.5 cm)
Commercial and hand-dyed
cottons, hand-painted silk, ribbon;
machine appliqué and quilted,
hand beaded; glass beads
Photos by D. James Dee

templates (enlarge 200%)

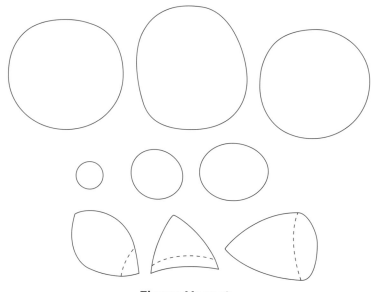

Flower Magnet

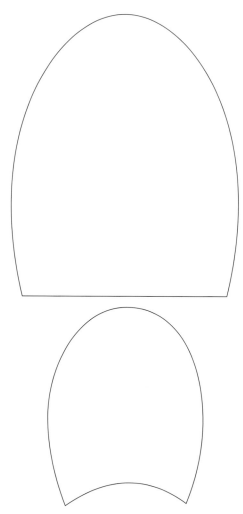

Latin Beauty

Hugs & Kisses Card

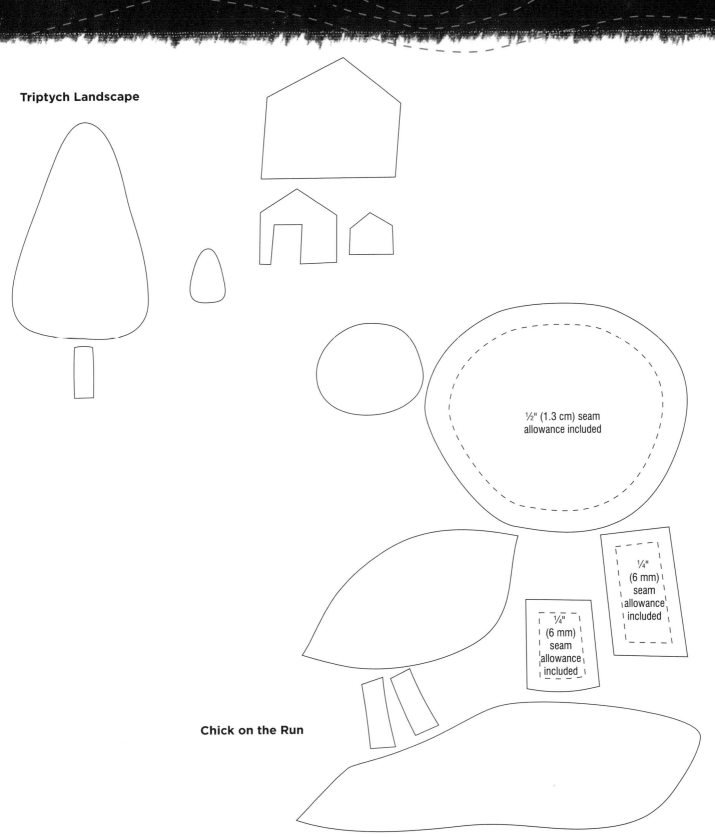

Triptych Landscape

½" (1.3 cm) seam
allowance included

¼"
(6 mm)
seam
allowance
included

¼"
(6 mm)
seam
allowance
included

Chick on the Run

templates (enlarge 200%)

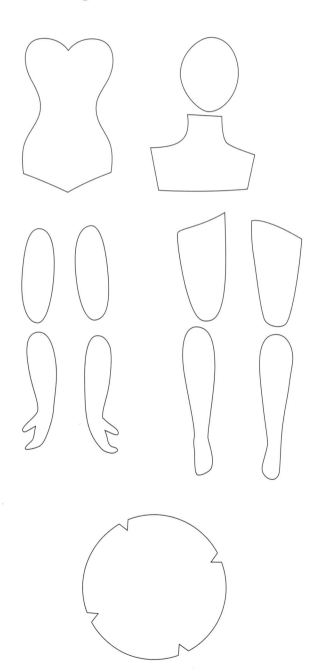

Reach for the Stars

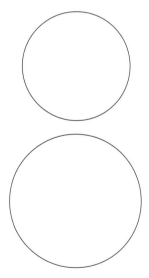

Flowers on a Hill

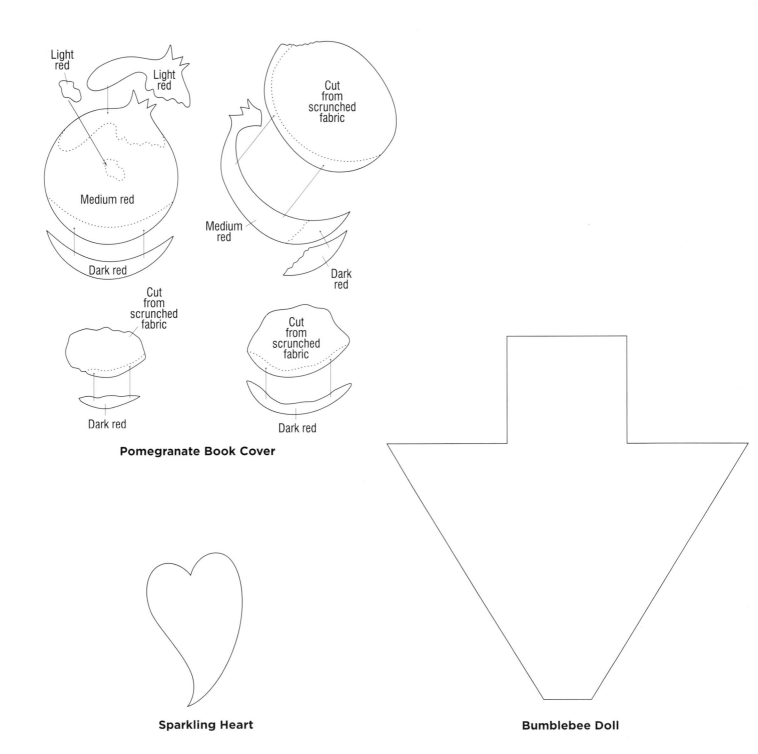

Light
red

Light
red

Cut
from
scrunched
fabric

Medium red

Medium
red

Dark red

Dark
red

Cut
from
scrunched
fabric

Cut
from
scrunched
fabric

Dark red

Dark red

Pomegranate Book Cover

Sparkling Heart

Bumblebee Doll

templates (enlarge 200%)

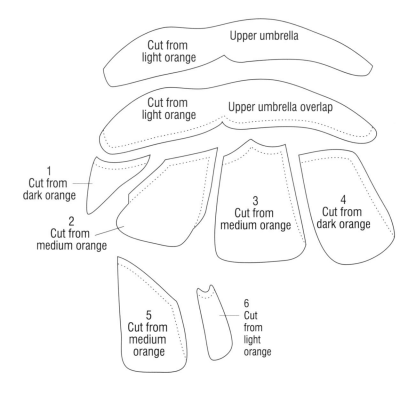

Umbrella Abstracted

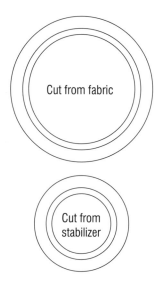

Jewels of Our Past

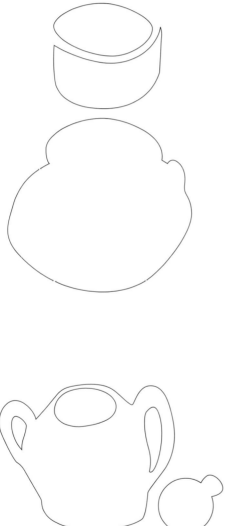

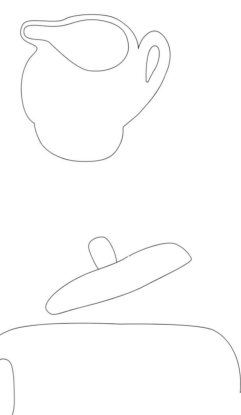

Tea Time Apron

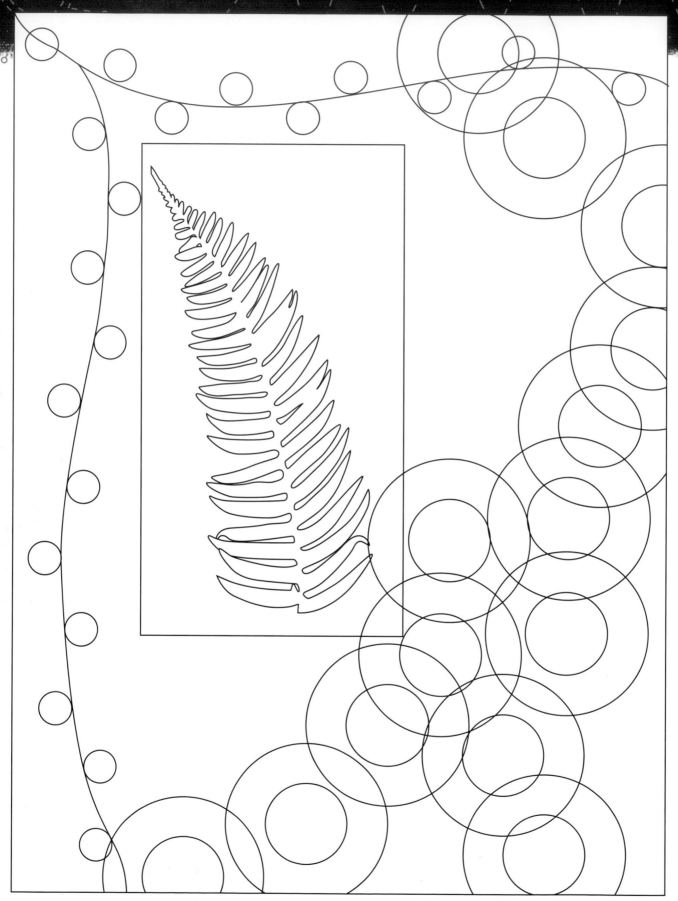

Forest Fern Embroidery Template (Enlarge 300%)

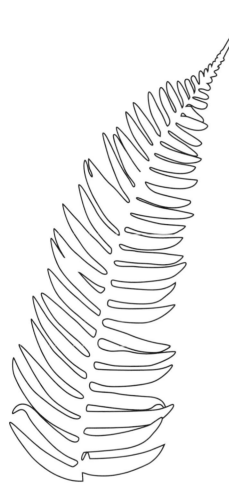

Forest Fern (Enlarge 300%)

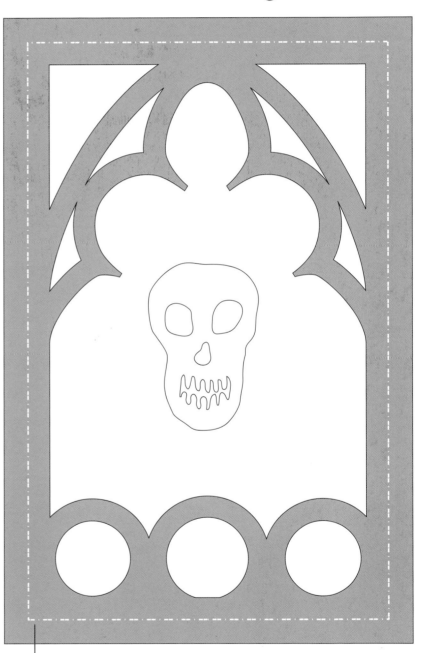

Fold under seam allowance on this line.

Horror Vacui (Enlarge 200%)

about the *designers*

Deborah Boschert lives in Lewisville, Texas, with her husband, two children, and their dog, Lincoln. She is a fiber artist who creates art quilts, fabric postcards, mixed media collages, and other bits of crafty goodness. Her work has been published in *Quilting Arts, Somerset Studio, Artitude*, and *Artella* magazines. Her art has also been displayed at quilt shows, galleries, and with The Frayed Edges, a small group of likeminded fabric fanatics whose goal is to share, encourage, and inspire one another. Deborah is a member of the Dallas Quilt Guild and Dallas Area Fiber Artists. Check out her blog about life and art at DeborahsJournal.blogspot.com. To see more of her work, go to www.DeborahsStudio.com.

Marné Cales has loved making things since the age of six, when she created a tiny purse from scraps of nylon. Barbie clothes soon followed. She watched her mother and grandmother quilt but had no interest in the craft until she was a teenager and decided to teach herself how to do it with the aid of a library book. She studied clothing and textiles in college, and her love of textiles continued to grow over the years. A technical writer by day, Marné cuddles up with one or more of her two cats and two dogs at night and creates everything from sweaters to quilts. She documents her creative life on her blog www.heylucy.net.

Kate Glezen Cutko is a mother, artist, and adoption social worker who lives in Bowdoinham, Maine. She is a member of Art Quilts Maine, The Frayed Edges, and the Bowdoinham Guild of Artisans. Her rural neighborhood on the shores of Merrymeeting Bay, her family, and her travels provide her with all the inspirational material she needs for her work. In her art quilts, Kate never does the same thing twice. She is constantly inspired by a new fabric, a new subject, a new found object, or a friend's shared inspiration.

Kathleen Daniels started out as a traditional quilter in the early 1980s. When she realized there was no wrong way to put pieces of fabric together to create a work of art, she turned to art quilts. Color is a major influence on her work. She also enjoys working with fabrics of different textures. Kathy is a member of Art Quilts Maine, the statewide organization of art quilters, and The Frayed Edges. Her work has been shown at sidewalk art festivals, gift shops, and small gallery shows. She also writes and shares her works in progress at her blog www.studiointhewoods.blogspot.com.

As a textile artist on the beautiful Oregon coast, **Julia Donaldson** is inspired by the natural world around her. With 18 years of experience, she works to exploit the unique properties of fabric and thread to create the rich textures that set textile design apart from other art forms. Julia enjoys incorporating unusual elements like shells, rocks, mosses, and wool/silk roving into her work. With work in both private and museum collections, she has had pieces accepted into national juried exhibitions and won many awards. Visit her website at julialdonaldson.com.

Marjorie Dade Lucas Kafader is a mother, clown, substitute teacher, garden designer, toy maker, and textile artist. Since 1981, she has been owner of a children's entertainment service in Wilmington, Delaware, using her talents and degree in textiles and clothing to make costumes for the business. The unifying themes of Marjorie's life are children and color. When not sewing or teaching, she can often be found with a paintbrush in her hand, recycling old furniture or garden items into colorful works of utilitarian art. You can find more of her work online at www.MarjorieDade.etsy.com.

Mavis Leahy grew up in a creative household, with an art historian for a mother and a musician for a father. She learned to sew on her mother's Singer Featherweight sewing machine and acquired her first quilt at the age of 10. Her love affair with quilts has continued through the years. Today, antique and vintage textiles are her passion. Through them, she feels a strong connection to the quilters, weavers, and artisans of long ago, whose textiles she uses in her work. To see more of Mavis's work, visit www.turkeyred.com.

Joan K. Morris's artistic endeavors have led her down many successful creative paths, including costume design for motion pictures and ceramics. Joan has contributed projects to numerous Lark books, including *Hardware Style, Hip Handbags, Beaded Home, Tops to Sew, Pillows to Sew, Curtains to Sew, Button! Button!*, and many more.

Heather Noblitt is a multi-media collage artist specializing in paper, jewelry, and fabric collages. She has had numerous works of art published in *The Stamper's Sampler* magazine and a featured article in *Rubberstampmadness* magazine. Heather finds much inspiration in vintage images and artifacts. By displaying her found treasures in clear glass jars she also finds inspiration with using color tone and contrast. Heather lives in Richardson, Texas, with her husband, Mark, and daughter, Sarah. To see more of her work, visit her online shop, Sunshine Designs Etc. at www.sunshinedesignsetc.etsy.com.

Veronica Hofman Ortega became interested in quilt making in the 1990s and has won awards for her quilts and wearables. Her work has appeared in national quilt and art exhibits, juried competitions, and publications. To support her fiber passion, Veronica has a formal education and a full-time career in graphic arts and printing technology. A transplanted Yankee from the south side of Chicago, she now lives with her husband, two dogs, and cat on a ridge in Chattanooga, Tennessee. She spends as much time as possible creating in her studio, Alpha Dog Designs, and can be reached electronically at vhofman@aol.com.

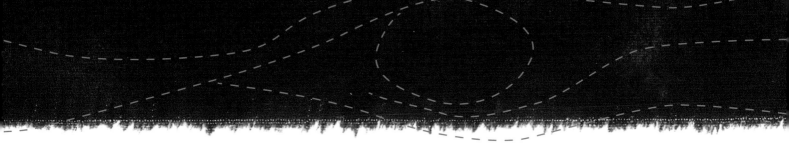

Jennifer A. Reis is a practicing and teaching artist who lives in Eastern Kentucky on a 100-year-old farm with sheep, goats, a variety of fowl, two cats, and one dog. She holds degrees in studio art and arts administration from Syracuse University, Columbus College of Art and Design, and Morehead State University, where she is gallery director and instructor of art appreciation courses. Her award-winning works have appeared in exhibitions across the nation and been featured at the Kentucky Museum of Art and Craft, the Artisans Center of Virginia, the American Quilter's Society Museum, Miami University Art Galleries, and the Southern Ohio Museum, among others. Publications and promotions regarding her work have been included in *Art in America, ArtForum*, and *Arts Across Kentucky* publications. More information about her work can be found at www.jenniferareis.com.

Christina Romeo is a multimedia artist with a strong pull toward textile design. As a child, she learned to cross-stitch, collage, and reconstruct clothes into abstract creations. After a 10-year career in the dental health profession, Christina now pursues art full-time, selling work throughout Canada and the United States and from her website. Her studio is located in the heart of the Selkirk Mountains, in Revelstoke, British Columbia. For more information on her work, visit www.jamtartbaby.com.

A graduate of Georgetown University's School of Foreign Service and The Fletcher School of Law and Diplomacy at Tufts University, **Sarah Smith** has worked for a U.S. Congressman in Washington, D.C.; volunteered in Guinea-Bissau with Operation Crossroads Africa; and served as a U.S. Foreign Service Officer. While assigned to the U.S. Embassy in La Paz, Bolivia, Sarah came across a discarded *Keepsake Quilting* catalog, which opened up the doors to the quilting world. Sarah now sells her work (www.sarahannsmith.com), teaches quilting, has a line of patterns, and is the author of the forthcoming *Unraveling Threadwork*, to be published by the American Quilters' Society (AQS). Sarah's quilts have been widely exhibited and published in the U. S. and Europe in both art and quilting venues, including the International Quilt Festivals in Houston and Chicago, the Quilt Expo in Lyon, France; and the American Quilters' Society show in Paducah, Kentucky.

Fabric artist **Sherrie Spangler** lives in northern Illinois with her husband and teenage daughter, as well as a rabbit, a flying squirrel, three parakeets, and assorted fish. Her vividly-hued art quilts and wearable art incorporate fabric that she paints, stamps, foils, and embellishes with beads, glittering thread, feathers, chocolate candy wrappers, and other objects. After 10 years of working as a newspaper reporter and editor, Sherrie retired to stay home with her children and put her passion for art and sewing to use. Sherrie has lectured about art quilting and has exhibited in galleries, museums and quilt shows nationally and internationally. Her work has also been featured in many publications. She can be reached at sherriequilt@yahoo.com.

Sue Spurlock lives in Carbondale, Illinois, and works as a licensed clinical social worker when she isn't creating art. She enjoys using hand needlework and embroidery and beads in her pieces—not as embellishments, but as integral parts of the images she creates. Her work has been featured in solo and group exhibits and won awards. Sue recently had a piece published in *Quilting Arts Magazine*. She can be reached at suespurlock@gmail.com.

Larkin Jean Van Horn is a mixed-media textile artist working on Whidbey Island, Washington. In addition to making her own creations, she serves as a teacher and lecturer for quilters, fiber artists, and beadworkers. She is the author of the book *Beading On Fabric*, and she has also published patterns for wearable art garments and fabric vessels. Her work has been displayed and won honors both regionally and nationally. She is a past President of the Pacific Northwest Needle Arts Guild and a founding member of the Wearable Art Study Group. She is also active in a small art quilt group called Three Uppity Women, which exhibits locally and participates in fundraising for humanitarian causes. To see more of Larkin's work, visit her website: http://www.larkinart.com.

Index

Fiona Hammond
Blossoms with Bling, 2007
7 x 4 1/2 inches (17.8 x 11.4 cm)
Fabrics, text-weight paper,
sewing and beading thread; sewn;
flat beads, seed beads
Photo by Lark Books

It's all on **www.larkcrafts.com**

Daily blog posts featuring needlearts, jewelry and beading, and all things crafty

Free, downloadable **projects** and **how-to videos**

Calls for artists and **book submissions**

A free **e-newsletter** announcing new and exciting books

…and a place to celebrate the **creative spirit**